Red State Revolt

The Jacobin series features short interrogations of politics, economics, and culture from a socialist perspective, as an avenue to radical political practice. The books offer critical analysis and engagement with the history and ideas of the Left in an accessible format.

The series is a collaboration between Verso Books and *Jacobin* magazine, which is published quarterly in print and online at jacobinmag.com.

Other titles in this series available from Verso Books:

Red State Revolt

The Teachers' Strike Wave and Working-Class Politics

ERIC BLANC

VERSO

London • New York

First published by Verso 2019
© Eric Blanc 2019

1 3 5 7 9 10 8 6 4 2

Verso
UK: 6 Meard Street, London W1F 0EG
US: 20 Jay Street, Suite 1010, Brooklyn, NY 11201
versobooks.com

Verso is the imprint of New Left Books

ISBN-13: 978-1-78873-574-2
ISBN-13: 978-1-78873-575-9 (UK EBK)
ISBN-13: 978-1-78873-576-6 (US EBK)

British Library Cataloguing in Publication Data
A catalogue record for this book is available from the British Library

Library of Congress Cataloging-in-Publication Data
A catalog record for this book is available from the Library of Congress

Typeset in Fournier MT by Hewer Text UK Ltd, Edinburgh
Printed and bound by CPI Group (UK) Ltd, Croydon CR0 4YY

CONTENTS

INTRODUCTION

In the spring of 2018, teachers and school staff across the United States fought back and won. By walking out for better pay and school funding, hundreds of thousands of educators etched their imprint onto the course of history.

The strike wave sparked by West Virginia produced a range of major victories. It also produced some great stories. While interviewing school employees during and after the walkouts, I'd always make sure to ask about their favorite moment of the struggle so far.

Some recounted the exhilaration of personally confronting a conservative politician. Many emphasized how proud they were of having become an organizer. Others told me about the joy of their first day back at school, when students thanked and high-fived them for taking a stand. More than a few were just relieved that they could now pay the rent.

I was particularly moved by stories about small acts of support from strangers. Abby Broome, a teacher in Putnam County, West Virginia, wrote to me about one such experience. Her letter poignantly describes how the strike imbued routine interactions with a spirit of solidarity:

> I was walking to my car probably 4 or 5 blocks from the state capitol. I was alone, have to admit kind of insecure as I'm a young woman and I was alone in unfamiliar territory and it was getting late. I was wearing my strike sign around my neck, had on my red bandana and red strike shirt. I passed a bus stop where a couple people were waiting for the shelter. Under different circumstances, I don't think any of us would have acknowledged each other. (We should have.) But this time one of the men spoke and said, "I support you. It's awesome what you all are doing. Keep fighting."
>
> Honestly, I was shocked. For weeks we had been ridiculed by some of our elected officials, the media, our own governor. But I learned that night that we had the support of hardworking people who know the struggle, working people probably having to take the city bus to work, people who fight every day to make ends meet, people who truly cared about what we were doing. It really changed things for me. I was tired like everyone else. I wanted things to get back to normal. But I felt energized and respected like I never had. I was proud. We were doing something bigger than ourselves. I think we were giving other people a little hope.

West Virginia's walkout gave hope to working-class people well past state lines. Inspired by the Mountain State strikers, school employees in Oklahoma, Arizona, and beyond followed suit. Confounding all expectations, these actions erupted in Republican-dominated regions with relatively weak labor unions, bans on public sector strikes, and electorates that voted for Donald Trump in 2016. And considering the fall 2018 work stoppages in Washington and a looming strike in Los Angeles, there is no sign that this militant educator upsurge will be short lived—nor confined to so-called red states.

This is a book about the power of strikes. It tells the story of the thousands of educators like Abby Broome who took workplace action for the first time and were profoundly transformed in the process. It's also a behind-the-scenes account of how militant teacher-organizers—most of them young radicals inspired by the 2016 Bernie Sanders presidential campaign—initiated these illegal rank-and-file rebellions and guided them to victory in alliance with their trade unions.

Finally, this book is an attempt to extract the main political lessons of the 2018 upsurge, the first wave of US work stoppages in multiple generations. Our side doesn't win very often; for decades, workers, organized labor, and the Left have been losing a one-sided class war waged by billionaires and their apologists. If we want to build an effective alternative to Trump and the Far Right, we can't afford to ignore the experience of the red state revolt.

A Historic Upsurge

At most times and in most places, the norm is working-class resignation, rather than resistance. But the first few months of 2018 were one of those rare instances in US history when ordinary people forced their way into the political arena, seeking to take their destinies into their own hands. In so doing, they transformed themselves just as much as they shaped their workplaces and society.

To quote Oklahoma teacher Gabrielle Price, educators "took a crash course in politics and government and will never be able to unsee what they have seen." There is more than a little poetic justice in the fact that many strikers belonged to the "white working class" that liberal elites blamed for Trump's election.

Teacher after teacher recounted to me epiphanies produced in the heat of struggle, ranging from disillusionment in Republican politicians to a newfound sense of individual and collective power. In the words of one Arizona educator: "Rallying at the capitol was one of few moments in my lifetime where I felt I stood exactly where one ought to—it was unequivocally purposeful, courageous and joyful."

Teachers and support staff were not the only ones to reach new political conclusions. Millions of workers in each of these states witnessed a major social battle in which workers, for once, came out on top. A whole generation of young people, in particular, just learned firsthand that mass action is both legitimate and effective. To quote Oklahoma high school student Ravi Patel, "Our teachers are setting an example of bravery by standing up to ignorance and inaction . . . Our teachers are setting a better example than our legislators have for the past decade."

To make these strikes a success, rank-and-file educators were obliged to step up in dozens of ways. Though labor unions played an important role in the walkouts, movement activities were often improvised from below, with all the strengths and limitations that this entailed. Their contributions included unglamorous tasks like making signs, collecting food for students, reading up on legislation, speaking with confused parents, texting a coworker to remind them to participate in the strike vote, or driving a group of peers to the capitol. Others actions required a bigger leap; for many teachers, this was the first time they'd made a speech at a rally, convinced coworkers to participate in a political action, spoken to the press, chaired a mass meeting, or confronted a politician.

In the span of a few months, tens of thousands of educators confronted and overcame personal fears, physical exhaustion, Republican bullying, and employer disciplinary intimidation. Initially, most doubted that a work stoppage was possible, because public sector strikes are prohibited in each of these states. As teacher Rebecca Garelli recalls, "People in Arizona were scared to rock the boat—and then West Virginia happened. All of a sudden, the catalyst was there. 'They're doing it, why can't we?'"

Though breaking the law was not a decision easily undertaken, teachers eventually embraced their defiance. Highlighting the long tradition of taking illegal action to win a righteous cause, many strikers made homemade signs that read, "Rosa Parks was not wrong." One West Virginia teacher posted the following to Facebook: "The way I look at it, Rosa Parks and Martin Luther King Jr. took a stand, I'd be in great company [if the state tries to throw us in jail]."

Legal threats were not the only ordeals they faced. In West Virginia, educators rallied for hours in the frigid rain; in Arizona, they marched and demonstrated in ninety-five-degree heat. Many also stressed the emotional turmoil associated with their participation in such a political rollercoaster. According to Azareen Mullins: "Our feelings were extreme from one minute to the next because of things that were happening inside the capitol doors. You'd feel exhilarated next to your chanting coworkers, but the very next moment you'd be crushed because of disappointing news from the Legislature. And then it'd start all over again."

The Supreme Court's anti-union *Janus* decision in June 2018—throwing all public employees back into the open shop era—has given the red state revolt an added degree of momentousness. Pundits across the political spectrum announced that *Janus* would be the nail in organized labor's coffin. But the walkouts clearly showed the potential for the revitalization of trade unions, even in the face of "right to work" laws and legal bans on strikes.

In fact, if the walkouts in Arizona, Oklahoma, and West Virginia are any indication, this Republican offensive may prove to be counterproductive for the ruling rich: by destroying the last remnants of public sector union security, the Supreme Court decision may thereby make militant workplace actions *more* likely. As a union lawyer for the American Federation of State, County, and Municipal Employees (AFSCME) warned the court on February 26, *Janus* risked raising "an untold specter of labor unrest throughout the country."

Though not all of their demands were met, striking educators in West Virginia, Oklahoma, and Arizona achieved more in the span of two months than had been won over the previous two decades. That they wrested these concessions from intransigent Republican administrations—who for years prior stubbornly insisted that there was no money available to meet the teachers' demands—made their achievements all the more significant. Both Oklahoma and Arizona, moreover, require legislative supermajorities to pass new taxes. Mass strikes have a remarkable knack for helping employers cough up concessions.

In West Virginia, the push for a work stoppage forced the state to freeze health care costs, cancel the imposition of invasive mandatory medical trackers, and drop both pro–charter school and anti-union legislation. Then, after almost two weeks of shuttered schools, West Virginia's legislature caved to the strikers and granted a 5 percent raise to *all* public employees—not only teachers. When I spoke with teacher leader Jay O'Neal in Charleston a few hours after victory was announced, he was ecstatic: "I'm thrilled, I feel like my life won't ever be the same again. It sounds like hyperbole, but it's not."

The gains won in Arizona were also impressive. Through two months of mobilization and six school days of strikes, the Red for Ed movement put sufficient pressure on the legislature to stop new proposed tax cuts, keep an anti-voucher referendum on the 2018 ballot, and win hundreds of millions of dollars in additional school funding. Teachers, moreover, obliged the state to grant them an immediate raise of roughly

10 percent, with the promise of another similar increase a few years down the line. No less importantly, Arizona's strike reversed Governor Doug Ducey's attempt to tie any funding increase to cuts from Medicaid, the arts, and students with disabilities.

The achievements of the red state walkouts were not limited to the formal policy arena. Even more important than gains in pay and funding were the advances toward revitalizing the trade unions and rebuilding a militant workers' movement. The illegal strikes in West Virginia and Arizona reflected, and spurred, a dramatic increase in working-class consciousness and organization, setting the stage for the conquest of further victories in the months and years ahead. To quote Garelli: "The movement and the walkout really increased people's political awareness and our level of grassroots organization. Fifty percent of the win here has been that we now have a strong, organized mass movement. And we're not going away. People now have the courage to fight."

In a marked reversal of fortunes for West Virginian organized labor, over 2,000 educators joined the unions in early 2018. Arizona—in which the union represented only 25 percent of school employees before the strike—experienced an even deeper sea change. Roughly 2,500 new members have joined. On a Facebook thread concerning the lessons of the strike, a teacher explained: "The word 'union' does not scare me anymore. I joined [the Arizona Education Association] and plan on continuing to fight for what is right for educators and students. I feel the most empowered I have ever felt as an educator and now do believe that change is possible."

This revolt shares important similarities with the last great round of rank-and-file radicalism in the United States, the strike wave of the late 1960s and early 1970s. But there are some critical differences. Whereas labor struggles four decades ago came in the wake of a postwar economic boom and the inspiring successes of the civil rights movement, this labor upheaval has erupted in a period of virtually uninterrupted working-class defeats and neoliberal austerity. As such, political scientist Corey Robin was right to call 2018's educator upsurge the "most profound and deepest attack on the basic assumptions of the contemporary governing order."[1]

The stakes are high. Public education remains one of the few remaining democratically distributed public goods in the United States. For that very reason, corporate politicians have done everything they can to dismantle and privatize the school system. As political economist Gordon Lafer documents in his book *The One Percent Solution*, this isn't only about immediate profits. Big corporations, he writes, are trying "to avoid a populist backlash" against neoliberalism "by lowering everybody's expectations of what we have a right to demand as citizens":

When you think about what Americans think we have a right to, just by living here, it's really pretty little. Most people don't think you have a right to healthcare or a

---

1 Corey Robin, "Striking Teachers Are 'Real Resistance' to 'Incoherent' Republicans and 'Gutted' Dems," interview by Amy Goodman, *Democracy Now!*, April 12, 2018, democracynow.org.

house. You don't necessarily have a right to food and water. But people think you have a right to have your kids get a decent education.[2]

Struggles to defend public education, in other words, have political implications that reach far beyond the schools themselves. Each of the teacher strikes raised the question of whether the tremendous resources of the richest country on earth should be used for meeting human needs or for deepening corporate profits. In a context marked by deepening social crisis and widespread popular anger, we should not underestimate the urgency of this issue. To counter the racist fearmongering of Trump and his supporters, moral condemnations are not enough. A credible political alternative must be provided.

Since West Virginia's strike erupted in February 2018, it's become clear that a new labor movement is not only necessary, but possible. To quote Arizonan music teacher and Red for Ed organizer Noah Karvelis: "The types of attacks we've seen in Arizona are common to the working class across the whole country. If educators in Arizona could stand up and fight back, anybody can stand up and do the same."

To the surprise of all, this frontal challenge to austerity and neoliberalism came in the form of illegal statewide strikes in Republican "right to work" bastions. Since unions in these states were relatively weak and collective bargaining

---

2 Cited in Lynn Parramore, "The Corporate Plan to Groom U.S. Kids for Servitude by Wiping Out Public Schools," *Institute for New Economic Thinking*, April 6, 2018, ineteconomics.org.

virtually nonexistent, the strikes took on an unusually volcanic and unruly form. In an unprecedented historical development, much of the organizing for these actions took place in secret Facebook groups where teachers could share their fears, hopes, personal stories, and action proposals (as well as countless silly memes). And with union officials reluctant to call for illegal mass action, rank and filers stepped into the leadership vacuum and filled it to the best of their abilities.

One of the main lessons from the red state revolt is that the Left needs labor just as much as labor needs the Left. Fortunately, socialists and the labor movement are beginning to overcome their decades-long divorce. In an interview conducted over celebratory beers, an hour after West Virginia strikers won their demands, Emily Comer—a socialist teacher, union member, and strike leader in Charleston—put it well: "If you have enough working people who are pushed to the breaking point, and who are angry about a specific grievance, then it's the duty of activists to let them know that they deserve better—and that their lives can get better if they take action on that issue. If you lead the way, people will respond."

This book describes the development of the strike wave through the words and perspectives not only of its rank-and-file participants, but also those of its main grassroots organizers. For both diplomatic and tactical reasons, activists in 2018 were reticent to publically speak about the internal conflicts that drove these movements forward. As such, the full story of their development has not yet been made public.

To understand how I was able to get this insider's take, some background information might be helpful. Last spring, *Jacobin* magazine sent me to be its on-the-ground correspondent for the strikes in West Virginia, Oklahoma, and Arizona. Truth be told, my journalistic credentials at that point were nonexistent. My parents are both union activists, and I was a high school teacher—and leftist public education organizer—in the Bay Area until 2017. Like so many of my colleagues, my meager teacher wages pushed me to go back to school; the strike wave popped off during my second semester as a doctoral student in sociology at New York University.

Upon arriving in each of the strike states, I'd immediately explain my personal-political background to the local organizers. I told them the truth, which was something to the effect of: "I've got to write some articles about what's going on, but, mostly, I want you all to win—so, please, put to me work if you can." Ultimately, I spent the bulk of my time organizing national solidarity for the strikers and talking politics with the core teacher activists over nightly beers.

The upshot was that, although I missed more than a few article deadlines for *Jacobin,* I ended up earning the trust of key rank-and-file leaders. They gave me access to their internal meetings, their secret Facebook groups, and even many of their personal texts. Without that inside information, there's no way this book would have been possible.

To supplement these personal observations and the abundant primary sources embodied in the Facebook groups, I scoured the local press and also interviewed over one hundred teachers, service personnel, organizers, students, union staffers and top officials, and superintendents. Politically, these individuals ranged from Trump supporters, to liberal trade unionists, to socialist cadre—and I suspect that each will agree and disagree with aspects of my analysis. Though this is an unabashedly partisan account, I've tried hard to remain scrupulously committed to the facts, fair to those I criticize, and critical of those I support.

And one final note on geography: This book deals with the West Virginia, Oklahoma, and Arizona strikes, which were by far the most important actions of the spring 2018 red state movement. The strikes in these three states were multiday work stoppages, unlike the one-day, mostly symbolic walkouts that took place in Kentucky, North Carolina, and Colorado. Likewise, I don't delve into the recent work stoppages in Washington and other blue states—these actions, developing as they did in Democratic-run regions where strikes are not illegal, merit their own separate study.

It's a welcome complication that by the time this book hits the shelves, there could very well be new educator struggles erupting in unexpected places throughout the United States. In the same way that teachers in West Virginia and Arizona learned from the successes of Chicago's 2012 school strike, the 2018 experience should be of considerable use to public education workers and their allies in these battles to come.

From Trump's vicious scapegoating to the looming threat of climate catastrophe, rays of political hope are few and far between. At this dangerous and volatile juncture in US history, it's easy to fall into despair. But the 2018 education strikes not only underscore the immense potential for mass working-class politics; they also provide important insights into how this latent power can be tapped.

Working people are angry and looking for alternatives to business as usual. In the least likely of circumstances, school employees in West Virginia, Oklahoma and Arizona rose up to deal a serious blow to the forces of reaction. For everyone across the country who is eager to do the same, there's no better place to start than by learning about the red state revolt.

THE ROOTS OF REVOLT

In West Virginia during the strike, the capitol became flooded with national reporters. And the number one question they'd asked us was: How could something like this happen in Trump country? My responses went back and forth from confusion, to exasperation, to anger. People are *desperate* in West Virginia. But the national media hasn't been paying attention to the conditions in our state that made the election of Donald Trump possible—the exact same conditions that made our strike possible.

—West Virginia teacher Emily Comer

Class struggle has a remarkable way of puncturing political myths, and for those willing to learn, the recent education strikes reveal important truths about American politics. Not least of these is the superficiality of the red state/blue state paradigm.

According to Republican and Democratic leadership alike, the United States is fundamentally divided between coastal bastions of liberal cosmopolitanism and a heartland of bible-thumping conservatives. Republicans see themselves as the voice of a traditional Middle America solidly committed to God, Life, and Country above all else. For their part, Democratic elites tend to write off much of the country as racist dupes brainwashed by Fox News. Simultaneously, the Democratic Party establishment brandishes the electorate's purported conservatism as justification for its refusal to embrace redistributionist policies such as taxing the rich to pay for health care, education, and other public services.

The 2016 presidential election seemed to vindicate these mirror images of bipartisan condescension. Despite the fact that most workers (white and otherwise) either abstained or voted for Hillary Clinton, it was largely the "white working class" that was held responsible for Trump's election. Frenzied liberals lamented the inability of white workers to recognize their own self-interest; for instance, the *Daily Kos* declared, "Be happy for coal miners losing their health insurance. They're getting exactly what they voted for."[1] Eminent liberal columnist Jonathan Chait was similarly blunt: "To watch Donald Trump and see a qualified and plausible president, you probably have some kind of mental shortcoming . . . What I failed to realize . . . is just how easily so many Republicans are duped.[2]

---

1   Markos "Kos" Moulitsas, "Be Happy for Coal Miners Losing Their Health Insurance. They're Getting Exactly What They Voted For," *Daily Kos*, December 12, 2016, dailykos.com.

2   Jonathan Chait, "Here's the Real Reason Everybody Thought Trump Would Lose," *New York Magazine*, May 11, 2016, nymag.com.

Commentators in the *Nation* concluded that "increasingly, class is simply not a meaningful dimension along which American politics is fought. Rather, the battle-lines are drawn around issues of racial identity and tolerance of diversity."[3] And in an essay titled "No Sympathy for the Hillbilly," liberal op-ed columnist Frank Rich insisted that trying to win over white workers through populist economic policies was "wishful thinking" given their "blind faith" in Trump. "Let them reap the consequences for voting against their own interests," he insisted. "Who are Democrats to stand in the way of Trump voters who used their ballots to commit assisted suicide?"[4]

In light of such assumptions about the cognitive abilities and political inclinations of Middle America, it should come as no surprise that the political establishment did not know what to make of the eruption of teacher walkouts in the heart of so-called Trumpland.

For their part, Fox News and the Republican Party did their best to ignore the strikes. In contrast, the representatives of official liberalism attempted periodically to provide an explanation for the walkouts. Their explanation was straightforward: Republican leaders imposed such low salaries that teachers were forced by circumstances to rise up. These work stoppages, put simply, were a spontaneous, collective response to particularly egregious conditions in a

---

3   Sean McElwee and Jason McDaniel, "Fear of Diversity Made People More Likely to Vote Trump," *Nation*, March 14, 2017, thenation.com.

4   Frank Rich, "No Sympathy for the Hillbilly," *New York Magazine*, March 20, 2017, nymag.com.

number of red states. As such, the strike wave was inherently limited in its geography (archconservative regions) and in its political goals (higher teacher salaries and the election of Democrats).

There are some grains of truth in this account. But on the whole, liberals have misidentified the key factors that made possible the 2018 education upsurge. To understand why these strikes erupted—and what they tell us about the obstacles and opportunities for labor militancy across the United States—we need to dig deeper.

Low Wages

Liberal analysts are right that the recent rebellions were in large part instigated by the dire conditions facing teachers. As sign-wielding strikers have made the nation aware, teacher pay in Arizona, Oklahoma, and West Virginia ranked, respectively, forty-seventh, forty-eighth, and forty-ninth in the nation.[5]

More than a few of these educators teeter on the edge of poverty. Nicole and Matt McCormick, for instance, are public school teachers in Mercer County, West Virginia, who have struggled for years to pay the rent without falling into debt. "We've got a constant fear of missing payments on our credit card and we've had real conversations about moving into a

---

5   National Education Association, *Rankings of the States 2017 and Estimates of School Statistics 2018*, Washington, DC: NEA, 2018. Unless otherwise noted, all statistics on teacher pay, state funding, school size, etc. come from this comprehensive NEA study.

camper. We often have to feed our four kids at McDonalds, and sometimes it feels like my fault," explained Nicole. "We're white-knuckling 'til pay day—the worst is when students are selling something in class for a fundraiser that you can't afford." One of Matt's viral Facebook posts on the eve of the walkout was a February 13 photo of his $1.14 bank balance, with the caption: "I call this portrait 'Two days until payday on a teacher's salary.'" Had the strike lost, the couple planned on immediately moving to another state. As Matt told me later, "We saw the strike as a last-ditch effort to stay in West Virginia."

Many educators have to work multiple jobs to survive. Among them, Oklahoma teacher Mickey Miller's experience is not atypical. During the day, Miller teaches at Booker T. Washington High School in Tulsa. After the school day is over, he works until seven thirty at the airport, loading and unloading bags from Delta airplanes. From there, he goes on to his third job, coaching kids at the Tulsa Soccer Club. "I have a master's degree, and I have to work three jobs just to make ends meet," he explained in April. "It's very difficult to live this way."

Each of the three states that experienced strikes in early 2018 is facing a severe shortage of teachers. Instead of attracting qualified educators by increasing pay and improving working conditions, districts have turned to hiring emergency-certified staff with no teaching degrees and little to no training. In Oklahoma, the number of such jobs for the 2017–18 school year stood at roughly 2,000. Arizona's shortage was even more serious, with 5,000 positions staffed by uncertified teachers.

Low wages are a central source of frustration. But contrary to the liberal account, the walkouts were not an automatic response by red state teachers to receiving the country's worst salaries.

First of all, the crisis of teacher pay—and public education generally—is hardly limited to a few regions. Middle America isn't a land apart; its problems are endemic to the country as a whole. To quote Arizona teacher Rebecca Garelli, "Everywhere is dealing with the same troubles. This isn't a crisis of a few states; it's nationwide. Teachers have been asked to do more with less for over ten years."

When adjusted for inflation, average US teacher pay decreased by 4 percent during the ten years following the Great Recession of 2008–2009. Roughly one in five teachers has to work second jobs during the school year. Unsurprisingly, the teacher shortage is a truly national crisis. Particularly since student debt to pay for rising college costs has skyrocketed, young people are looking for employment in better-paid fields. As of fall 2017, unqualified instructors fill over 100,000 teaching spots, and 40 to 50 percent of new teachers quit within five years, making the US teacher attrition rate two to three times higher than that of countries like Finland and Singapore.[6]

Though it is understandable that red state strikers have highlighted their position at the bottom of the US pay scale, national salary-ranking systems actually obscure the fact that

6   Desiree Carver-Thomas and Linda Darling-Hammond, *Teacher Turnover: Why It Matters and What We Can Do About It*, Palo Alto: Learning Policy Institute, 2018.

teachers receive *similarly low* wages across the country. On the face of it, the mean 2017 salary of $79,128 in second-ranked California appears to be almost double that of the $45,292 average in Oklahoma. Yet when adjusted for the cost of living, California drops to twenty-fifth, Oklahoma rises to thirty-fifth, and the pay gap between the two states plummets to less than $4,000. Recent studies show that most of the country actually converges in terms of real teacher pay, and that five of the bottom ten are blue states.[7]

Wage disparities would be even narrower if average salaries were disaggregated to particular school districts. Within many states, teacher pay—like per-pupil funding—differs dramatically between cites, as roughly half of school revenues comes from local property taxes. Astronomical housing costs in many blue cities make it next to impossible for many teachers to pay rent, let alone buy a home. Average rent in San Francisco is 700 percent more expensive than in Wichita, yet teacher pay is only 40 percent higher in the former. With 664 unfilled spots going into the 2016–17 school year, San Francisco Unified School District—employing only 3,600 teachers—came close to the 725 vacancies that West Virginia as a whole experienced last year.

Liberals overemphasize pay rankings because they misunderstand the roots of working-class struggle under capitalism. There's a common conception that if workers are not resisting, it's because they're too well off. But more poverty

---

7　Michael Winters, "Where Do US Teacher Salaries Really Go the Furthest?" *EdSurge*, June 1, 2017, edsurge.com.

doesn't usually lead to more resistance. In the United States and across the world, workers with relatively better wages, job security, and working conditions have always tended to be overrepresented in labor struggles and organizations because they have greater power, resources, and confidence to resist their exploitation.

Labor grievances typically emerge not from *absolute deprivation*, but from *relative deprivation*: that is, from the gap between what working people believe they deserve and what they have. This gap is especially wide for teachers in the United States, who receive 20 to 30 percent less in pay than similarly educated workers—a far-greater disparity than in other industrialized countries. "Both me and my wife have higher education degrees," explained Matt McCormick. "So getting paid what we do is a real slap in the face."

The worst-off layers of the working class are rarely the most organized or most militant. Consider the differences in pay between striking teachers and other workers in their regions. The average yearly salary of a West Virginia teacher in 2016 was $45,240, while the median earnings in the state were $27,543. Disparities were similar in Arizona ($48,020 versus $30,096) and Oklahoma ($42,460 versus $29,038). As is usually the case, relatively better-off wage earners struck back first.

When it comes to working-class struggle, the idea of "the worse, the better" is neither politically, nor morally, justified. The recent work stoppages, for instance, arose once the economy started to rebound, not when conditions were at their absolute worse. Unlike in the immediate aftermath of the Great Recession, state revenue streams have improved somewhat between 2014 and 2018, providing public employees with hope that collective action could realistically deliver concessions.

And, as is generally the case with strike activity, low unemployment helped counter widespread fears that a walkout would result in mass firings. As one Oklahoma educator argued in a March 19 Facebook debate over the risks of striking: "Lose our jobs? They have no one to replace us with."

Working and Learning Conditions

Most representatives of the status quo—including the corporate media, state governments, and the Democratic and Republican Parties—have done everything possible to frame the recent walkouts in the narrowest-possible light. By myopically emphasizing salary issues, these mainstream accounts of the struggle have largely overlooked the centrality of other social grievances in stoking collective resistance.

Opposition to the decimation of public education and the devaluation of teaching as a profession has been a central driving force of teacher resistance in red states and blue states alike. For instance, the 2012 Chicago teachers' strike—a pivotal inspiration for radical leaders of the red state revolt—primarily concerned issues like class size, equity, standardized testing, and school closures. And in Oklahoma and Arizona, demands for increased school funding were at the very center of the 2018 walkouts. Salary demands were also decidedly secondary in West Virginia's strike, where the movement arose primarily in response to proposed changes to the state's public health insurance plan, the Public Employees Insurance Agency (PEIA).

It's crucial to understand that teaching is much more than a job for many educators. They see their work as a calling—one that has been systematically undercut by politicians and bureaucrats, high-stakes testing, underfunding, and privatization. It was not mere rhetoric when strikers in each of these states chanted, "We're doing it for the kids!" Teachers at rallies, in school meetings, and over Facebook denounced politicians for devaluing education standards by hiring uncertified and untrained individuals, cutting funding, raising class sizes, and imposing excessive standardized tests. To quote a March 19 post from Oklahoma's main teachers' Facebook group: "Pawnee is also in. It's exciting to see the list [of districts agreeing to strike] get bigger! Fighting for the education of our students and the respect for the profession [fist emoji]."

Like most labor battles, these strikes were about winning respect as much as anything else. More often than not, fights around pay are simultaneously struggles for basic human dignity; economic demands are rarely *only* economic. In the words of one irate West Virginian teacher on the eve of the walkout, "We are *human beings*." Azareen Mullins of Charleston, West Virginia, described the cynicism that came from years of work without respect, explaining how "most new teachers at [her] school don't last through the fifth year."

Mullins spoke for many teachers when she explained that there was also a gendered dimension to the strike: "One of the reasons that they have been able to keep our pay levels so low is that it's a female profession, largely. If it were a male-dominated profession, I don't think we'd be treated in the same manner. Looking in the sea of faces during the strike, it was mostly women. A lot of the activism we've seen is not necessarily feminist, but it's female driven."

What used to be treated as a middle-class profession has been steadily subjected to job intensification and deskilling. Studies consistently show that the most common reason for leaving teaching is not the lack of pay, but rather excessive testing and accountability measures, followed by dissatisfaction with school administration. For decades, the classroom autonomy and creativity that teachers need to provide quality education to students has been under steady bipartisan attack. In a recent Gallup poll, 93 percent of teachers affirmed that they should have "a great deal" or "a lot" of input in school decisions. Only 31 percent, however, feel that they have it.

Increased work for stagnating pay has become the norm in teaching, as it has in so many other sectors of the economy. Student enrollment has risen by close to 1.5 million in the decade following the recession, yet in 2017 there were 135,000 fewer public school employees than in 2008. Broader cuts to public services have put increased responsibilities on educators to act as de facto counselors, mental health advisors, and food pantry staff for students in need.

"Our teachers are so taken for granted, but they do so much for us, they really go out of their way to help," noted

Morgan Smith, a high school junior from Seth, West Virginia. "If students are going hungry, they'll always try to help get them a bag full of food to take home."

Charleston teacher Emily Comer described this dynamic from an educators' vantage point: "As teachers we have a unique window into the entire economy of our communities, so every day we see the effects of the opioid crisis, poverty, students experiencing trauma. The worse the economy gets, the harder my job gets; it's more stressful with more emotional burden on the teachers in my building, who are mostly women."

Demands on behalf of students were especially prominent in Oklahoma and Arizona, where calls to restore school funding were by far the most central nonwage demands of the strikes. A decade of harsh austerity has devastated their already-underfunded public education systems. Between 2008 and 2017, per-pupil instructional funding was cut by 28 percent in Oklahoma and 14 percent in Arizona, ranking them as the forty-sixth and forty-ninth lowest-funded states in 2017. Like decreasing pay, these rollbacks are part of a national trend: twenty-nine states provided less per pupil in 2017 than they did in 2008.[8]

Due to budget cuts, many districts in Arizona and Oklahoma have been forced to reduce the school week to four days—in the latter, 18 percent of districts now follow this condensed schedule. Class sizes are often enormous,

8   Michael Leachman, Kathleen Masterson, and Eric Figueroa, "A Punishing Decade for School Funding," *Center on Budget and Policy Priorities*, November 29, 2017, cbpp.org.

while textbooks are scarce and scandalously out of date. Innumerable arts, language, and sports programs have been eliminated. Broken desks, crumbling ceilings, chair shortages, and rodent infestations have become normal. For Christy Cox—a middle school teacher in Norman, Oklahoma, who has had to work the night shift at Chili's to supplement her low wages—reversing these school cuts was her main motivation to walk out: "The kids aren't getting what they need. It's really crazy. Though the media doesn't talk about this as much as salaries, I feel that funding our schools is the primary issue."

Far from being inevitable, today's funding crisis is the direct result of decades of policies prioritizing big business over working people. Since 1990, the Arizona legislature has cut taxes every year but one. In Oklahoma, where taxes have not been raised by the legislature since 1990, $1 billion in revenue has been lost yearly due to the tax cuts pushed through since the early 2000s.

By the eve of the walkout, Oklahoma had the United States' lowest tax rate on oil and gas—not a minor issue in a state that is the country's third-largest producer of natural gas and fifth-largest producer of crude oil. At a student rally during the walkout, Southmoore High School student Ravi Patel thus made the case that Oklahoma was undergoing a priorities crisis rather than a funding crisis: "Don't let them tell you that funds don't exist. They're sitting right on them. Those sitting on Capitol Hill shouldn't be building themselves a hill of capital. We need to stop putting profits above pupils . . . From this day onwards, legislators will fear us hashtag-wielding teenagers more than they fear the oil and gas companies."

As in the rest of the United States, spending cuts have gone hand in hand with a push for privatization. The corporate playbook is not complicated. First, you starve public schools; then, you insist that the only solution to the artificially created education crisis is "school choice"—meaning privately run (but publicly funded) charters, as well as vouchers for private schools. In Oklahoma, there are now twenty-eight charter school districts and fifty-eight charter schools. "Is the government purposely neglecting our public schools to give an edge to private and charter schools?" asked Tulsa teacher Mickey Miller.

Without doubt, it is in Arizona that this nationwide offensive to take education out of the public sphere has advanced furthest. Over the past two decades, the archconservative billionaire Koch brothers and the American Legislative Exchange Council (ALEC) have spent millions financing efforts to privatize Arizona's public education system. In 1997, Arizona pioneered a program granting individual and corporate tax credits to fund private school tuition. As ALEC explained in a recent tribute to Arizona's vanguard privatizing efforts:

> Arizona is not only solidifying its place at the top of the ALEC Report Card on American Education ranking, but showing the rest of the country that educational choice doesn't have to be limited to being a lifeline for a few students, trapped in the worst the public education system

has to offer. Instead, Arizona has offered Americans a vision of a totally new world.[9]

About 17 percent of Arizonan students currently attend a charter school—more than three times the national average. Some of these charters generate millions of dollars in private revenue. Like many other parents in Arizona, Dawn Penich-Thacker questioned the state's priorities: "If there's so little funding for education, why should it be given to profit-making businesses?" In 2014–15, for example, charter schools made almost $60 million for Basis, the private corporation that services its school franchise.

As is generally the case with attacks on working people, privatization has had a disproportionate impact on working-class communities of color. As a result, Arizona's schools have become increasingly segregated: though 44 percent of students in Arizona are Latino, they make up only 36 percent of charter students.

Private charter schools aren't the only institution receiving funds that could be going to education or other public services. Arizona has one of the highest incarceration rates in the nation, disproportionately locking up Latinos and African Americans. With an annual expenditure of approximately $1 billion—over 10 percent of the state's total budget—the Arizona Department of Corrections was among the few state agencies to continue to receive funding increases after the

---

9   Inez Feltscher Stepman, "Arizona Leaps into Innovative Educational Future with Universal ESAs," *American Legislative Exchange Council*, April 12, 2017, alec.org.

recession began. The situation is even more dire in Oklahoma, where one in one hundred adults is in jail or prison—the highest incarceration rate in the world, dwarfing any other US state or foreign country. In such a context, widespread calls by Oklahoma educators and parents to "Fund schools, not prisons" took on particular urgency.

Resignation and Resistance

On March 25, 2018, a *Tulsa World* editorial argued that "given the recent history of [cuts and low pay in] Oklahoma it isn't remarkable that teachers are planning to strike. What's remarkable is that it didn't come sooner."[10] This raises an important, broader question: Why have these attacks on public education been allowed to go on for so long?

The main liberal answer, as we have seen, is that the majority of people in red states are too dumb or racist to understand their own interests. According to this logic, if governmental policies are bad, it's the fault of the voters who elected bad politicians to office. In a 2015 *Washington Post* article entitled "Why the Voters Are to Blame," influential centrist journalist Jennifer Rubin declared:

> We can and we should blame voters. *Someone* is listening to all that talk radio and talking-head cable news . . . We get the politicians, campaigns and media we deserve. If we

---

10 "After Years of Legislative Failure, Oklahoma Teachers Are Ready to Strike," *Tulsa World*, March 25, 2018, tulsaworld.com.

want all three to be better, we need to stop embracing the worst of each.

This argument entirely overlooks the gulf between the democratic ideals and the actual practices of the US state. Sadly, there's little correlation between the political desires of most Americans and the policies implemented by elected officials.

The main cause of this dramatic political disjuncture is not hard to find. Countless studies have demonstrated how the inordinate wealth and power of corporations and the ultrarich systematically distort our democratic process. As Martin Gilens demonstrates in his important monograph *Affluence and Influence: Economic Inequality and Political Power in America*, "When preferences between the well-off and the poor diverge, government policy bears absolutely no relationship to the degree of support or opposition among the poor."[11]

The vast majority of the US population supports raising taxes on the rich and corporations to pay for strengthening public services like public K–12 and higher education, health care, social services, and infrastructure.[12] A majority of workers would vote for a union at work, were they given the opportunity, and roughly 80 percent of working people believe that the economy unfairly benefits the wealthy.[13] Nor

11   Martin Gilens, *Affluence and Influence: Economic Inequality and Political Power in America*, Princeton: Princeton University Press, 2012, 81.

12   Meagan Day, "The Myth of the Temporarily Embarrassed Millionaire," *Jacobin*, March 23, 2018, jacobinmag.com.

13   Alex Rowell and David Madland, "The Working-Class Push for Progressive Economic Policies," *Center for American Progress Action Fund*, April 17, 2018, americanprogressaction.org.

are these majoritarian progressive views limited to economic issues: in 2018 polls, 75 percent of Americans said they believe immigration is good for the country, only 29 percent said it should be decreased, and over 64 percent said that racism is a "major problem" in the United States.[14]

Contrary to what liberal pundits would have us believe, the dynamic is remarkably similar in Republican-led states. A poll of the South found that a strong majority support raising taxes to improve schools. Indeed, strengthening K–12 and higher education came in as a top priority for voters, second only to the economy and jobs.[15] And in each of the three states that struck in 2018, polls have for years revealed major-itarian support for raising teacher salaries and increasing taxes to pay for public education.

At this point, a skeptic might ask: If workers are so left leaning, then why haven't they voted progressive politicians into office? The short answer is that they have tried to do this for decades. Yet time and time again, Democratic Party poli-ticians have broken their campaign promises and imple-mented regressive policies, thereby setting the stage for the return of (undoubtedly worse) Republicans to power.

Many people have forgotten that the neoliberal turn of the late 1970s was initiated by the Jimmy Carter administration

14   Niraj Chokshi, "75 Percent of Americans Say Immigration Is Good for Country, Poll Finds," *New York Times*, June 23, 2018, nytimes.com; Andrew Arenge, Stephanie Perry and Dartunorro Clark, "Poll: 64 Percent of Americans Say Racism Remains a Major Problem," *NBC News*, May 29, 2018, nbcnews.com.

15   Jackie Mader, "Poll Finds Southern Voters Want More Education Spending," *Hetchinger Report*, February 13, 2018, hechingerreport.org.

as well as by Democratic governments on a city- and state-wide level. Bill Clinton furthered this trend in the 1990s by passing the North American Free Trade Agreement (NAFTA) and gutting welfare programs. More recently, Barack Obama and the Democratic-led Congress responded to the Great Recession by bailing out the banks instead of working people, dashing the hopes of their base and paving the way for the Republicans' sweep of the House in 2010 and the election of Trump in 2016.

On the question of public education, Obama and then–secretary of education Arne Duncan continued, and in some case deepened, many of the worst education policies of their Republican predecessors, including high-stakes testing, merit pay, and charters. In the wake of the 2008 recession, Democratic governors, state legislatures, and mayors pushed through severe austerity measures, and in numerous states they even actively supported laws to roll back teachers' union power.

A lack of popular enthusiasm for the Democrats in Oklahoma, Arizona, and West Virginia is not surprising, given their track record while in power. For instance, in 2006 Arizona's Democratic governor, Janet Napolitano, partnered with the Republican-dominated legislature to push through $500 million in tax breaks. And in Oklahoma, some of the first major tax cuts for the rich and corporations began in 2004 under Democratic governor Brad Henry and a Democratic-led Senate. Royce Sharp—director of the forthcoming documentary *The Reddest State*, on Oklahoma's leftist history—argues that the two-party system has obscured the actual political priorities of working people: "Looking at Oklahoma's election results isn't a very good indicator of ordinary people's politics because the Democratic Party is bought by massive international corporations just as much as the Republicans. Here in Oklahoma, politics is really more about top and bottom than it is about Right and Left."

Experiences in Appalachia are even more illustrative of the trajectory of the Democratic Party and why its fealty to corporate America has turned so many formerly blue states red. West Virginia was run by Democrats from 1932 straight through 2014, when Republicans took control of the state legislature for the first time in over eighty years. Though the decline of the all-important coal industry was a development beyond the Democrats' control, the same cannot be said of their response to the ensuing social crisis.

The roots of the party's spectacular implosion—and West Virginia's current health care woes—can be traced back to 2006 when then-governor Joe Manchin and his Democratic majority in the legislature imposed a set of devastating tax cuts, costing the state roughly $220 million in yearly revenue. In subsequent legislative sessions, Democratic lawmakers proceeded to cut the corporate net income tax from 9 to 6.5 percent as well as eliminate the business franchise tax. Rather than acknowledge their unswerving loyalty to out-of-state energy companies, Joe Manchin and other top Democrats argued that Republican-lite policies were necessary because of the conservative inclinations of West Virginian voters. In the words of one party leader, "You can't really blame Joe [for his moderate approach]. You can blame West Virginia."[16]

Blaming West Virginia's voters for their purported conservatism became a national media obsession after Trump decisively swept the state in the 2016 presidential elections. Reporters descended onto Appalachia to paint a picture of the strange hillbilly natives who helped propel Trump to the White House. Yet, as was true in the rest of the country, a large majority of people in West Virginia either abstained or voted for Democrats. Indeed, only 38 percent of registered West Virginian voters cast their ballots for the Republican candidate.

The minority of workers who *did* vote Trump often expressed their motivation explicitly as opposition to an intolerable status quo. In a Facebook discussion on the first day of the walkout, one Mingo County teacher explained, "I never voted for Trump, I voted against Clinton." Only months earlier, many of Trump's voters had cast their ballot for the socialist candidate Bernie Sanders—who won every single county in the West Virginia Democratic primary.

The absence of a credible mass political alternative to the twin parties of capital goes a long way toward explaining why there's been relatively little pro-education advance in the electoral arena, with the notable exception of the Sanders insurgency. But it doesn't directly answer the *Tulsa World*'s question about why we haven't seen more teacher walkouts.

---

16 Cited in Michael Kruse and Burgess Everett, "Manchin in the Middle," *Politico Magazine*, March/April 2017, politico.com.

One important reason for the low number of work stoppages in general is that US labor law is uniquely set up to prevent these. With the most draconian strike restrictions of any advanced capitalist democracy, the United States is out of compliance with most of the fundamental international standards established by the International Labor Organization. "Labor laws in this country are formulated for labor to lose," noted mine worker leader Richard Trumka before he became the decidedly more moderate head of the American Federation of Labor and Congress of Industrial Organizations (AFL-CIO).[17]

Labor law is stacked against workers across the whole United States, not just in red states. Numerous media commentators have mistakenly asserted that teachers in West Virginia, Oklahoma, and Arizona could not legally strike because they lived in "right to work" states. In actuality "right to work" laws don't address strikes or union formation; rather, they allow workers in unionized workplaces to avoid paying union dues. Such laws are certainly anti-labor, but they are just the tip of the iceberg. Few people realize that teacher strikes are banned in most of the country: they're legal in only twelve states. And even in these exceptional areas, public sector work stoppages are often subjected to strong restrictions.

Workers, in short, are up against serious institutional roadblocks and powerful enemies. In the absence of a

---

17   Cited in Joe Burns, "A Strategy Based on Strikes Means Breaking the Law," *Labor Notes*, April 16, 2013, labornotes.org.

militant labor movement that projects a viable alternative to the status quo, it should come as no great shock that there haven't been more walkouts. Political acquiescence is more common than resistance because workers tend to search for individual solutions to collective problems, particularly where labor organizations are weak. "Until very recently, Oklahoma teachers have been going without any hope, feeling like nothing could be done to change things," observed Mickey Miller. "People would say, 'It is what it is; it's out of our power.'"

The risks of illegal public sector walkouts are very real, as famously demonstrated by President Ronald Reagan's watershed 1981 firing of 10,000 Professional Air Traffic Controllers Organization (PATCO) workers. Educators, like other workers, are understandably reluctant to participate in actions that could potentially cost them the job upon which they and their families depend. Fear and resignation are mutually reinforcing.

The prevailing illegality of teacher strikes can be traced back to the stunted outcome of the last public employee upsurge, four decades ago. Unlike in most other capitalist democracies, the United States prohibited unions, strikes and collective bargaining for all public employees throughout most of the twentieth century. This unhappy state of affairs was suddenly challenged in the 1960s and 1970s when a massive wave of militant, illegal work stoppages by teachers and other public sector workers swept the country.

With both political momentum and numbers on their side, threats of mass firings did little to dissuade the strikers. This unprecedented upsurge put politicians from both parties on the defensive. For a time, winning full rights to strike and collectively bargain appeared to be a goal within reach for public employees. Yet Democratic and Republican lawmakers were cunning. In most states they tied their concession of collective bargaining rights to the continued prohibition of work stoppages—now with the additional specification of penalties like financial fines or union decertification (which proved to be more enforceable than mass firings).

Rather than keep up the struggle until the right to strike was cemented, public sector union leaders accommodated themselves to the new institutional arrangement. Winning this truncated form of collective bargaining was a mixed blessing: it allowed teachers' unions to grow relatively strong, it established decent job stability, and it enabled some significant material victories. But at the same time, it drastically narrowed the scope of workers' collective power and militancy, thereby setting the stage for labor's current crisis. Having won a "seat at the table," public sector union leaders began actively enforcing strike prohibitions from the 1980s onward. As the labor movement lawyer acknowledged during courtroom debates over the 2018 *Janus* decision: "Union security is the tradeoff for no strikes."

West Virginia, however, was exceptional in this regard: public employees in the state have neither the right to strike, *nor* to collectively bargain. As such, Mountain State educators had no institutional recourse to give vent to their growing indignation at year after year of rising health care costs. In the short term, this led to resignation and demoralization.

As late as December 30, 2017, posts like the following were common on Facebook: "Teachers, by and large, are a passive bunch (In WV they don't even vote in mass). There is at present no real sign of any major action on their part."

But like a pressure cooker with no escape valve, the steady buildup of anger created the conditions for a social explosion. In February 2018, after months of organizing by a small core of radical rank-and-file activists, the state finally erupted. For educators across West Virginia—and across the country soon after—the day of reckoning had arrived.

2

THE POWER OF STRIKES

Since the strike, there's a definite sense of solidarity that wasn't there before. When you go in to school and see all of your coworkers in red, it's like they're saying, "I'm with you, I got you." It's hard to even sum up that feeling. You used to go in to school, do your thing, and go home. Now if there's a struggle, we go do something about it because we're in it together. It's not just that there are a lot more personal friendships—we saw that we had power.

—Arizona teacher Noah Karvelis

When it comes to political strategy, there's no need to reinvent the wheel. West Virginia and the other recent teacher revolts have confirmed the continued relevance of an old political insight: *strikes are workers' most powerful weapon.* Formerly accepted as commonplace, organized labor dropped this idea decades ago; on the Left, it has been marginalized. For both movements, the consequences of turning away from on-the-job militancy have been dire.

Labor-management "cooperation" has led to concession after concession by unions across the country. The much-heralded organizing model associated with the Service Employees International Union (SEIU) and with the "New Voice" leadership that swept the AFL-CIO in the 1990s has not significantly increased union density. Nor has the prevailing form of social justice unionism reversed organized labor's decline. Even today's progressive unions often focus more on electing and lobbying Democrats than on building workplace fightbacks.

The union movement's turn away from the strike over the past four decades has reinforced the Left's drift from organized labor. As unionization rates and job actions continued to drop, it was understandable—if strategically shortsighted—that progressives and radicals would look for greener political pastures elsewhere.

New social movements since the 1960s, such as environmentalism, feminism, and LGBTQ liberation, have scored important victories, but none have approximated the social weight of organized labor at its height. Demonstrations, civil disobedience, and electoral campaigns haven't been enough, on their own, to reverse the neoliberal tide. In the absence of a strong labor movement capable of challenging capital and the state, organized radicals have remained marginal—and movements against oppression and environmental devastation have been unable to generate the social strength necessary to extract their most far-reaching demands.

The red state revolt illustrates why the Left needs labor to win—and why bringing back the strike is an indispensable and urgent task for anybody interested in creating a better world. Paralyzing production remains the most impactful and empowering action that working people can undertake. Since the system depends on our labor, we have immense structural leverage. This holds true for public employees—including predominantly female workforces, like teachers—no less than it does for the private sector.

With an eye to understanding the power of strikes, this chapter explores how the work stoppages unfolded in West Virginia and Arizona. Since Oklahoma took a different path, it will be discussed mostly in the following chapter.

I begin by outlining the processes and mechanisms through which educators tapped into their latent power—as well as the obstacles they confronted along the way. From there, my focus turns to an analysis of how the strikes radically transformed the collective organization, self-confidence, and political consciousness of working people. As Polish socialist Rosa Luxemburg once noted, "Those who do not move, do not notice their chains."

What Education Strikes Do

Like all strikes, a walkout by governmental employees (such as teachers) aims to shut down a given workplace in order to extract concessions from their employers. The basic means to do so is the same as in a private company: get as many workers as necessary to withhold their labor. Fittingly, one of the most popular chants of strikers at West Virginia's capitol was, "If they don't fix it, shut it down!"

If only a fraction of people strike, or if demoralized strikers begin to return to work, strikers cannot effectively paralyze production in a particular work site or sector. For this reason, in both private and public sector walkouts, building some form of collective organization (i.e., a trade union) and upholding unity in action between different workers is almost always a precondition for success. To sustain coordinated strike action around common demands, a workforce therefore needs to sufficiently overcome internal divides regarding occupation, religion, politics, nationality, race, or gender.

The immediate target of a public employee strike (the state), however, is by definition distinct from that of a private sector walkout (a business). Flowing from this are some important strategic consequences. Most obviously, public employees don't generally have the power to directly halt capitalist profits by withholding their labor. Educators play an indispensable role in the reproduction of capitalism: we train the workers of the future. But the absence of profit-halting power is one important reason why the revitalization of organized labor cannot be limited to the public sector.

At the same time, capitalists aren't neutral bystanders in state employee work stoppages. Business leaders—who use their immense economic power to ensure that governmental policy corresponds to their interests—know that walkouts for better social services often result in profit losses through higher taxes. Successful strikes also cut against capital's drive, in its endless search to increase profits, to privatize the public sector. Finally, the powers that be are well aware of the threat of contagion: public employee strikes risk inspiring job actions inside private enterprises.

So while work stoppages by state employees are an *indirect* challenge to big business, their leverage doesn't come from paralyzing profits. Rather, public sector strikes win by creating a social and political crisis. Closing schools, for instance, creates a crisis for governmental leaders, who are charged with providing this essential service to the public. Politicians who are unable to resolve the conflict on terms supported by the electorate risk getting voted out of office.

School strikes affect students, too, who need an education to get a job or get into college. Many also depend on schools for meals and supervision. Additionally, teacher walkouts often create havoc for parents because somebody needs to care for their kids while they're at work.

Paralyzing an essential government service, in other words, puts pressure on the state, as well as on those layers of the population to which that service is provided. In her 2016 book *No Shortcuts: Organizing for Power in the New Gilded Age,* union strategist Jane McAlevey notes that in public education, like health care, "the point of production *is* the community."[1] For this very reason, the question of winning and maintaining public support is indispensable in any teachers' strike.

Aiming to win over parents and the broader public, each of the contending sides will naturally seek to blame the other

---

1 Jane McAlevey, *No Shortcuts: Organizing for Power in the New Gilded Age,* New York: Oxford University Press, 2016, 28.

for the conflict. For example, a typical conservative op-ed published a few days before Arizona's strike called the impending action a "war against parents":

As of Thursday, the fight will no longer be teachers vs. politicians; the fight will be teachers vs. parents . . . Some parents are begging friends and family to watch their kids. Others are getting prices for daycare and worrying if they'll be able to afford it on their stretched budgets.[2]

Faced with such arguments, striking educators invariably reply that these hardships were caused by the administration's refusal to meet their reasonable demands. In making this case to the public at large, educators have an important advantage over their employers: they can lean on their established relationships with parents. Thus, what teachers lack in power to cut off profits, they can often make up for through their influence among broad layers of the working class.

Christine Campbell, president of the American Federation of Teachers—West Virginia (AFT-WV), put it well: "The thing that makes the public sector different is the relationships we develop. Educators are embedded in our communities; people trust us to educate their kids. So when parents see the teachers of their children struggling to make ends meet, working at a second job on the weekend, this is a much more

---

2   Jon Gabriel, "If Arizona Teachers Strike Now, It's a War against Parents, Not Politicians," *Arizona Republic*, April 24, 2018, azcentral.com.

direct relationship with the community than in the private sector."

Public education's location at the heart of social reproduction means that these work stoppages involved far more people than the roughly 130,000 teachers and support staff that struck in Arizona, Oklahoma, and West Virginia. The total number of students that missed class was well over 1.5 million, and the number of affected family members roughly twice that. So even if we don't include the one-day walkouts in Kentucky, Colorado, and North Carolina, it's clear that the red state rebellions involved many millions of individuals.

To sum up: the basic challenge for a successful education strike is to close schools by building up and maintaining employee unity in action, while simultaneously seeking public support. Hostile politicians and their proxies will try to reverse these processes, aiming to prevent a walkout or to force educators back to work before their demands are met. To see what this looked like in practice, let's begin by examining the role of the strike's opponents.

Attacks from Above

While right-wing opposition to educators took on distinct forms at different moments in each strike, overall the dynamic conformed to that famous saying (wrongly attributed to Gandhi): "First they ignore you, then they laugh at you, then they fight you, then you win."

Until very recently, politicians from both major parties generally ignored the demands of teachers in Arizona,

Oklahoma, and West Virginia. Rather than frontally argue against pay and funding increases, state leaders pled poverty, claiming that the money just wasn't there. The state met annual union-led "Lobby Days" with a polite, if stubborn, rebuff.

Once momentum toward a strike started picking up in early 2018, it became difficult for state leaders to continue ignoring educators. Upholding claims about empty government coffers, Republicans began to openly mock those who dared to demand change. In Oklahoma, Governor Mary Fallin infamously declared to the press that teachers were acting like "a teenage kid that wants a better car."

For his part, West Virginia Governor Jim Justice told teachers to trust him and not be "dumb bunnies." In protest, incensed educators soon began showing up at the capitol wearing bunny ears. Across the country, Arizona Governor Doug Ducey fired the first shot in what would soon become an especially vicious smear campaign against the state's teacher leaders. In early April, Ducey justified his refusal to meet with Red for Ed representatives, calling their movement a "political circus." He accused twenty-three-year-old teacher leader Noah Karvelis of being a Democratic Party "political operative" seeking to undermine Ducey's November bid for reelection. "The idea that I'm a political operative is absurd," Karvelis explained during the strike. "I'm a K–8 music teacher—I literally spend all day singing with a puppet on my hand."

It's worth noting that sustained organized opposition to the strikes came virtually only from above. Notwithstanding the liberal media's exaggerated claims about the reach of protofascist movements in Trumpland, grassroots right-wing groups were a negligible force in these events. Nicole McCormick, a public school teacher in West Virginia, recalls that there were "very few antis" during the work stoppage: "We had a counterprotester one day at our picket line, but since she had a red sign, people thought she was with us."

Far more consequential was opposition to the strikes from leading forces within the school system itself. Charter school administrations, for one, were prominent in undermining the work stoppages. Though a handful of charters participated in the walkouts, most openly scabbed.[3]

But charters weren't the only element undermining the public education movement from within. Statewide superintendents in West Virginia and Arizona, unlike many of their district-level peers, also openly opposed the strikes. One week before West Virginia's educators walked out, State School Superintendent Steve Paine issued the following declaration:

Work stoppages by public employees are not lawful in West Virginia and will have a negative impact on student instruction and classroom time. Families will be forced to seek out alternative safe locations for their children, and our many students who depend on schools for daily nutrition will face an additional burden.

---

3   Eric Blanc, "Arizona Versus the Privatizers," *Jacobin*, April 30, 2018, jacobinmag.org.

Republican Attorney General Patrick Morrisey made a similar announcement:

> A work stoppage of any length on any ground is illegal. Let us make no mistake, the impending work stoppage is unlawful. State law and court rulings give specific parties avenues to remedy such illegal conduct, including the option to seek an injunction to end an unlawful strike.

This remained their position over the entirety of West Virginia's strike, during which they repeatedly—and unsuccessfully—threatened educators to return to work.

In Arizona, the situation was similar. Hoping to prevent a walkout, State Superintendent Diane Douglas spoke on every television and radio show available, announcing that teachers could lose their jobs by walking out.

These threats succeeded in scaring many educators, particularly in the lead-up to the strikes. On social media and in break rooms, teachers expressed their worries about getting fired, suspended, or fined. One Arizona teacher recalls: "Tensions were running high across the state. Almost every educator I knew was nervous and unsure of what would happen." Others worried about paying the rent and grocery bills once the strike began. As Mary Wykle, a West Virginia bus driver, explains, "Up until the very day the strike began, we had no idea that the superintendents would end up shutting the schools and paying us by treating the walkouts like snow days."

Despite incessant threats against educators, it's significant that at no point did politicians or administrators impose legal or financial penalties on the strikers. The red state revolt was never obliged to confront full-scale state repression. How should we make sense of this governmental reluctance to move from words to deeds?

One explanation put forward in the media for why educators were not legally penalized is that these were superintendent-supported "walkouts," not real strikes. It's true that local superintendent and school board support was significant. For instance, by closing the schools ahead of time, district leaders enabled full-time school employees to continue to get paid during the strikes, since they could make up the missed days later in the year. Some district superintendents sincerely supported the movement's demands because devastating cuts and teacher shortages made it more difficult for them to do their jobs. Nevertheless, superintendent and school board support was more uneven than described in the media. And the fact remains that, in West Virginia and Arizona at least, these *were* strikes—and illegal ones at that. Whatever the personal inclinations of different district leaders, the initiative for the work stoppages always came from below. Indeed, it was only under pressure that the schools closed, after workers voted to shut them down.

In West Virginia, most organizers and workers assumed from the start that the superintendents would not agree to a work stoppage voluntarily. Union organizer Allen Stump explains that the educators presented district leaders with an ultimatum: "Basically, we said to the superintendents: We have over 90 percent of your employees announcing that they're not coming in to work. So either you cancel school or you'll have a bunch of students and nobody will be there— which would be a huge safety issue for the kids."

Even the most supportive superintendents acknowledged this dynamic. Mingo County's Don Spence, the first superintendent in West Virginia to agree to close his schools, explained to me why he had made this decision: "I saw the teachers' unity and determination; that's why I closed our schools. I didn't set out to do anything. They did the work. They deserve all the credit. All I did was support."

In Arizona, though not every single district struck, the general course of events was similar. As Arizona Educators United leader Dylan Wegela puts it, "*We* called the strike vote—we didn't consult with the superintendents about this ahead of time." Most district leaders were public about this fact, as seen in a letter to parents from Deer Valley Unified School District: "If a strike is planned, DVUSD will make every effort to avoid closing schools. We are currently working on plans to keep our schools open in the event of work stoppage. However, if we have too few staff members to safely hold school, we may be forced to close schools." Numerous superintendents attempted to intimidate employees into remaining at work, and once the strike began, many tried to pressure their staff to return.

In both West Virginia and Arizona, Republican leaders had more than enough legal justification to punish striking educators; indeed, strikes throughout US history have been broken on far-flimsier legal grounds. And despite the support of some local superintendents, the state's highest governmental bodies were clear about the illegal nature of these work stoppages. Arizona Superintendent Diane Douglas directly addressed the question: "It is illegal to strike in Arizona, and by every definition I've read, this is a strike." Douglas openly rejected claims that because "the [school] doors were closed" by local superintendents, teachers' actions did not qualify as a strike. She was not wrong to note that "the doors would have never been closed if the teachers didn't vote to walk out."[4] For all of these reasons, it's clear that superintendent sympathy was not a primary reason why the government did not resort to repression.

Another explanation of the government's legal inaction was that the teacher shortage tied the politicians' hands. According to this argument, which was shared by many in the movement, the state couldn't take repressive action against teachers because it had no one to replace them with. Though it's clear that the shortage undercut many educators' fears about getting fired, this line of reasoning is unconvincing. Even had there been no educator shortage, the sheer number of employees on strike would have made it very hard to fire all strikers. Moreover, state officials had many means to break the strikes other than mass dismissals, including the imposition of steep fines on individuals or organizations, union decertification, and firing (or jailing) the strike leaders.

---

4   Cited in "Arizona Teachers Group Challenges Idea That Walkout Is an Illegal Strike," *KTAR News*, April 30, 2018, ktar.com.

None of these measures, however, were imposed in Arizona, Oklahoma, or West Virginia.

In fact, the main reasons governmental leaders avoided punishing the strikers were, above all, *political*: first, repression risked emboldening (rather than intimidating) the strikers and their supporters; and second, it risked further alienating politicians from the public. Unlike in the corporate world, a large layer of employers in the public sector—governors, legislators, statewide superintendents, and local school board members—are generally subject to popular reelection, which tends to make them take public opinion more seriously. Given widespread public support for educators during the 2018 strike wave, it's unsurprising that politicians and superintendents (who are chosen by elected school boards) were reluctant to resort to repression.

This brings us to one of the big lessons of the red state rebellions: at moments of mass struggle, legality comes down to a relationship of forces. If a strike has the organization, momentum, and support of the public at large, it's more difficult for the ruling elite to crack down. When asked in a post-strike press conference why he hadn't tried to impose an injunction, Superintendent Paine's reply was refreshingly honest: it would have only "added gas to the fire," he acknowledged.[5] In the words of West Virginia teacher Emily Comer: "It doesn't matter if an action is illegal if you have enough people doing it."

---

5   Cited in Jake Jarvis, "State Superintendent Reflects on Teacher Strike," *State Journal*, March 14, 2018, wvnews.com.

This is not a new phenomenon. In the public employee upsurge of the 1960s and 1970s, the state also found it difficult to impose legal penalties against strikes that were well organized and well supported. After the American Federation of State, County, and Municipal Employees (AFSCME) defied a 1968 injunction, its militant president, Jerry Wurf, explained: "I have never been impressed with the injunction. If you got the power to win the strike, it's academic. If you ain't got the power, they are going to knock your head off anyway."[6]

Wurf was also right to stress the dangers of striking without sufficient strength. In 2005, for instance, a poorly organized strike by New York City transport workers resulted in the jailing of their president, a $2.5 million fine, and the end of automatic union dues deductions. The red state revolt also witnessed some similar, if smaller scale, setbacks. In a story that deserved far more coverage, seven bus drivers in Georgia's Dekalb County were fired after leading their coworkers in a three-day wildcat "sick-out" in late April 2018.

As these defeats in New York and Georgia show, public sector strikes are not a silver bullet; *calling* a strike and *winning* a strike are two distinct tasks. To organize an illegal strike and win requires strong internal unity and external support.

The relationship of forces between labor and management, moreover, depends not only on workers' strength, but also on the strength of their adversaries. In West Virginia, for

---

6 Cited in Joe Burns, *Strike Back: Using the Militant Tactics of Labor's Past to Reignite Public Sector Unionism Today*, New York: Ig Publishing, 2014, 147.

instance, Republican politicians and state managers were caught somewhat flat-footed by the unexpected popular upsurge. By all indications, the powers that be were unprepared for the challenge. But by the time the strike wave reached Arizona in April, the Koch Brothers' anti-worker apparatus was well oiled and prepared for battle. The means through which workers and their unions were able to successfully confront these powerful opponents is the subject to which we now turn.

Workplace Unity

If the red state rebellions had one strategic watchword, it was *unity*. Organizers and rank and filers endlessly insisted that it was only by coming together across their myriad of divides that school employees could achieve their demands. The names of the Facebook organizing groups that launched the walkouts are indicative: West Virginia Public Employees United, Oklahoma Teachers United (OTU), and Arizona Educators United (AEU). In West Virginia, the page quickly became known simply as United.

This consistent emphasis reflects a basic fact about labor struggles under capitalism: namely, that as atomized individuals, workers are virtually powerless at work. Only by joining together with our coworkers in common organizations and actions are we able to assert ourselves against management.

The unitary ethos that characterized the school strikes was a far cry from the sterile sectarianism, political insularity, and callout culture that still prevails among so many on the Left. This divergence has a structural basis: building unity at the workplace is a qualitatively different task than it is in self-selecting social movements.

We don't choose our coworkers. Often all we have in common with them is our shared position of subordination to management. As such, effective labor organizing obliges constant engagement with people with very different backgrounds and belief systems. This is particularly true for strikes, which to succeed usually require exceedingly high levels of participation and coordination from a given workforce.

Once educators began seriously considering the prospect of walking off their jobs in early 2018, they quickly confronted the basic challenge at hand. On March 5, the first day of Arizona's Facebook group, one teacher immediately stressed the centrality of unity: "We do need to be united or it won't work. It has to be all or most. WV is a right to work state but because of the numbers of teachers that striked it worked." In support, she received the following reply: "Unity is the key guys. If it's just a few of us, they can pick us off one by one. But if we stand strong in the masses, they can't do jack."

It would be no easy task to bring together tens of thousands of school employees, who were divided and hierarchically stratified in dozens of ways. This was true even in West Virginia, with its strong regional identity, labor traditions and compact geography. Widespread disunity was evident in the United page's first debates over striking. In a January

7 thread initiated by Jay O'Neal on the lessons of the 1990 West Virginia teachers' walkout, he asked, "Do you think it's worse now than it was before the strike in 1990?" He received this reply: "Getting there. This is why a strike would be hard to pull off now because they play groups against each other."

Overcoming these divisions required a tremendous amount of political debate, both in person and online. Over the course of months, politics became the normal topic of conversation in lunchrooms, staff meetings, and normally apolitical community events. Each of the states' Facebook groups witnessed an endlessly unfolding discussion over whether a strike was possible, how to get there, what to demand, and how to win.

As important as these debates were, unity was above all forged through deeds. An effective buildup to something as risky as a strike required a whole series of smaller preliminary actions to generate working-class self-confidence and cohesion. For instance, AEU's first action proposal was for educators to wear red on Wednesday, March 7—a proposal that caught on and was repeated every Wednesday for the rest of the school year. Soon afterward, AEU leader Rebecca Garelli called on educators and allies to draw education facts and red markings on their cars; within days, Arizona's streets and highways were filled with Red for Ed messaging.

Rallying at the state capitol proved a particularly powerful means to bring educators together. On Facebook, one Arizona teacher expressed a commonly shared sentiment:

"The experience at the Capitol was incredible. I think that educators have been pitted against each other for so long (elementary vs. middle vs. high school; certified vs. classified, etc.) that to see that kind of unity and solidarity was amazing. It's easy to feel alone in this line of work, and being at the capitol reminded us all that we're not alone."

In many ways, it was this sense of joyful community that brought people back to the capitol day after day. In addition to marching and chanting all day, they shared snacks, stories, sunscreen, and phone chargers. People got used to talking for hours with strangers, as if this was an everyday occurrence. "It's like I've made 75,000 new friends," read a teacher's post from Phoenix. At times, one caught a small glimpse into what a society founded on genuine reciprocity might look and feel like.

To build these sorts of solidarity-generating mass actions, educators had to confront a whole series of obstacles along the way. To begin with, they were divided between union and nonunion members. A minority of public school employees in Arizona and Oklahoma were unionized—only 25 percent in the former, and 40 percent in latter. Among charter schools, union organization was virtually nonexistent. In West Virginia, roughly 70 percent of teachers belonged to the unions, but relatively few members participated in any active way.

Since labor organization is a crystallized expression of working-class unity, weak trade union organization in these states was a troubling indication that atomization largely prevailed. Though organized labor has succeeded in beating back some of the Republicans' worst attacks since 2014, most educators have for years treated the unions as, at best, a distant and ineffective third party, useful mostly for providing some form of insurance in case of individual trouble with administrators.

Even among organized educators, intra-union division was the norm in Oklahoma, Arizona, and particularly West Virginia. Unions compete, often viciously, for members. In the Mountain State a given school might have members of all three of the states' unions—the American Federation of Teachers-West Virginia (AFT-WV), the West Virginia Education Association (WVEA) and the West Virginia School Service Personnel Association (WVSSPA).

Communication, let alone collaboration, was the exception rather than the rule. Indeed, overcoming this paralyzing turf war was a primary motivation behind Jay O'Neal and Emily Comer's creation of West Virginia Public Employees United in October 2017. After months of rank-and-file pressure from below, the unions finally started collaborating in late January 2018. Crucially, the school-site strike votes in mid February included participation by all school employees, regardless of union affiliation.

Regional differences were another key challenge. Nicole McCormick recalls the situation preceding the strike: "I felt really isolated here. I was isolated not only as a teacher, but even from other people in the education system. Each school, each school district, felt disconnected from the others. West Virginia has a sense of cultural community—we love our sports teams, our foods (like pepperoni rolls), our mountains—but there was basically no political links or discussion across county lines."

Bridging these divides became an urgent necessity, since the attacks on the Public Employees Insurance Agency (PEIA) were coming from the state capitol in Charleston and because the salary schedule in West Virginia (as in Oklahoma) is determined at the state, rather than district, level. Again, the United Facebook page served as the main vehicle for rank-and-file educators to link up with their coworkers. "The United group became like one big faculty room where we could connect with other teachers and workers throughout the state," notes Ashlea Bassham, a teacher in rural Logan County.

By late February, West Virginia's movement had become truly statewide, as immortalized in its slogan, "55 united, 55 strong." Every evening of the strike, workers across the state would obsessively check the Department of Education website to see whether all other counties had voted to go out the next day. Educators ceaselessly stressed their pride that each of the state's fifty-five school districts had come together.

Katie Endicott from Mingo County describes this well: "I remember the first time I heard the '55 united, 55 strong' chant, I broke down and cried. Because it was unity like I had never experienced. We were up in front at the capitol, near the front of the Senate chanting and I remember someone just started holding hands, my hands. And it was people from Mason County, Putnam County, people I had never met before—but these were my brothers and sisters, these were my fellow educators. And we were standing together, we were standing united. And no one wanted to be the county that made it fifty-four."

Achieving this level of unity proved to be more difficult in Oklahoma and Arizona, neither of which experienced a complete statewide shutdown. One reason for this is that unions and labor traditions were significantly weaker than in West Virginia. Another was the sheer number of school districts in Oklahoma (512) and Arizona (715); while all cities and big towns in these states were paralyzed by the walkout, remote rural districts often remained aloof.

But given the size of Oklahoma and Arizona, the weakness of their unions, and their lack of continuity with past labor battles, the remarkable aspect of their strikes was not their relative geographic narrowness in comparison with West Virginia, but rather their statewide breadth. For unlike most education strikes in recent memory, these work stoppages were not limited to just one school district. In a country where labor law divides private and public sector workers into the narrowest-possible bargaining units, each of these strikes demonstrated the power of a more expansive approach.

Schools were closed for roughly 70 percent of students in Oklahoma, and 75 percent in Arizona—no small feat in so-called Trumpland. Unlike in West Virginia, collective bargaining in these two states exists in limited forms within some districts, creating a structural pressure to focus on localized targets. But, inspired by West Virginia's example, rank-and-file leaders in Oklahoma and Arizona focused their fire and their demands on the state government in order to coalesce as broad a movement as possible. "We could have organized on a district-by-district level," observes Noah Karvelis, "but it wouldn't have had the same power."

Divergent political perspectives were another source of division. Far from representing an ideologically homogeneous bloc, the movement was comprised of registered Republicans, Democrats, independents, and a small but influential layer of socialists. Estimates from education union organizers concerning the affiliation of their memberships were roughly the same in each of the states: Democrats (45 percent), Republicans (40 percent), and independents (15 percent and growing). In the past few decades, differences over issues like guns, abortion, and religion have divided the political loyalties of these red state educators. A large number of others, including many registered Democrats and Republicans, dismissed party politics altogether, viewing it as a corrupt game over which they had no control. For every teacher who voted for Trump, there was at least one who had nothing but the harshest possible things to say about the new president.

Had educators attempted to make broad ideological agreement (or a long list of demands) a precondition for unity in action, their movements would never have gotten off the ground. Instead they focused on the big, burning demands that the vast majority of school employees and community members already felt strongly about. Emily Comer underlines this as one of the big lessons of West Virginia's strike: "For a successful mass movement, people don't have to agree on partisan politics, on religion, or anything else for that matter. But they *do* have to come together and fight in solidarity around a shared issue. We've learned that people will push the other differences aside in the name of solidarity."

In West Virginia, Oklahoma, and Arizona, an organic, bottom-up emphasis on unity was so strong that participants generally avoided discussions of internal differences, whether in regard to ideology, gender, race, or religion. For instance, when I asked strikers about the particular challenges facing female teachers and strikers, they almost always responded by pivoting the conversation, insisting that the salient feature of the movement was that it united all educators, all public employees, or working people generally.

Among strikers there was also very little discussion of race. For the most part, the reason for this was simple: educators from all backgrounds actively sought to put their divergences aside for the sake of winning common goals. But in light of the centuries-long centrality of white supremacy in the United States and the prevailing liberal discourse about the racist "white working class," it's essential to explore racial dynamics between teachers in more depth.

In part, this relative silence on racial differences arose from the fact that a majority of strikers were white. Stephanie Price, a Black educator in Oklahoma's overwhelmingly white teaching force, explains that most of her coworkers did not fully appreciate the particular challenges facing communities of color in her state: "Racism is very much a problem in Oklahoma, and it's not really discussed. People here honestly don't realize the ways that they're racist. My town was a sundown town not that long ago—but people don't know that history or how it still shapes us today."

It was in large part due to experiencing "insensitive, borderline racist" incidents at work that she joined the Committee for Racial and Ethnic Minorities of her local union chapter: "Unfortunately, the state removed the cultural competence courses that we used to have. And it's not uncommon for me to get stopped in the hall at school by random teachers asking me why Black people are always overreacting to things, or telling me out of the blue that structural racism isn't a thing. The way I see it, the main form of racism today is different than people marching around with tiki torches—it's ignorance about what people of color in this country are facing."

During the red state revolt, proactive anti-racism among white educators was certainly not commonplace. Teacher unions and public schools in each of these states—like in the rest of the country—have had an uneven record, at best, when it comes to the struggle against racial oppression.

Nevertheless, most of the core rank-and-file leaders—particularly the socialists—were committed anti-racists, as were various top union officials. The fact that they didn't try to include demands against racial discrimination as points of unity for the walkouts did not mean that they saw such issues as politically unimportant. In fact, movement organizations and leaders were periodically denounced by right-wing forces for their public commitment to the struggle against xenophobia and racial oppression. For example, as proof of the Oklahoma Education Association's supposedly "far-left agenda," one conservative local news columnist seeking to discredit the walkout denounced the union's open support for immigrant rights.[7]

This line of attack was particularly widespread in Arizona. A *Breitbart* hit piece on Noah Karvelis condemned him for using "Black Lives Matter ideology in his teaching which, he tweets, allows him to connect 'black identity' to political 'activism' for his students."[8] And House Representative Maria Syms ratcheted up the racist dog whistle smear campaign:

> You would likely not want your children boarding his intellectual ark—or sitting in his exotic classroom . . . He prides himself on teaching the hip hop music of Kendrick Lamar (whose lyrics include "we hate Popo [police], wanna kill us dead in the street for sure . . .") to 10-year-olds, indoctrinating them in "social movements and societal change" and "socioeconomic and racial privilege."[9]

Karvelis's outspoken advocacy around these issues was an exception among teachers. But it's important to underline that these strikes showed that the blind spots, or unconscious prejudices, of white educators did not prevent them from

---

7   Dave Ruthenberg, "The Union Behind the Walkout," *Enid News and Eagle*, April 11, 2018, enidnews.com.

8   Susan Berry, "Arizona Elementary Teacher Leading Strike: 'Teaching Is Political,' " *Breitbart*, April 24, 2018, breitbart.com.

9   Maria Syms, "#RedForEd Leaders Are Not As Nonpartisan as They Claim," *The Arizona Republic*, April 24, 2018.

striking with their nonwhite coworkers for common demands. To quote Jacqueline Gilliard, an African American teacher in Mercer County, West Virginia: "There are a lot of Trump supporters and racists here in West Virginia. But I was totally included in the movement; I didn't feel any racism during the strike. You know, my next-door neighbor is a Trump supporter, but she stood right next to me on the picket line. I guess we were able to unite because we had a common goal— if it meant being a little uncomfortable, or being around someone you weren't used to being around, that was okay. Plus, as a teacher you're already used to working with a lot of different people all the time, because you have to do what's right for the kids."

Each of these movements was self-consciously inclusive of all educators, parents, and students. Vanessa Arredondo-Aguirre—a teacher in Yuma County and a top AEU leader—explains: "I never felt that I, or the Hispanic population, was being left out at all. Actually, my ideas for organizing Hispanic educators and parents were generally supported. I felt very included." Stephanie Price recounted a similar experience in Oklahoma: "I know we need to be tying social justice into education struggles, but honestly I personally didn't see instances where racism played a role in the outcome or process of the walkout."

Participation in multiracial struggle helped break down existing divides within workplaces. Educators from all backgrounds stressed this dynamic. For instance, Roz Ellis, a Black teacher at South Charleston High School, characterizes the strike as follows: "That was the most amazing experience of my life. It was so much better than 1990. Everyone was truly in it together this time. It didn't matter the color of your skin, it didn't matter your differences, everybody stood beside each other."

The consistently multiracial quality of these strikes was an indispensable aspect of their success. Tens of thousands of African American and Latino educators were active participants and leaders in all facets of the movement. In Arizona, Native educators spread the work stoppage to the reservations under the slogan "Rez for Ed," and they spoke in their native languages at the rallies in Phoenix. Latino educators, who constitute 14 percent of the state's teachers, were a particularly prominent force. Arredondo-Aguirre explains the dynamic: "It made a big difference that I was in the AEU leadership team—parents and other teachers saw that we were represented. A majority of teachers statewide are white, but there are still a lot of us. Lots of folks were speaking in Spanish—and when I spoke on stage at the rallies I made sure to speak in Spanish. So the movement was definitely not just white teachers!"

One of the ironies of the media's one-sided vision of racist Trumpland is that it has tended to make workers of color like Arredondo-Aguirre invisible. Liberal pundits, and even many left activists, strangely continue to assume that people of color are somehow not particularly interested in labor struggles or economic demands. But nonwhite teachers in these states were undoubtedly just as committed as their white colleagues to the fight for better pay, working conditions, and school funding.

Indeed, polls of Oklahoma teachers who left the profession found that educators of color consistently felt even more strongly about low pay than their white counterparts.[10] In the words of Price: "I think anytime you start talking about getting more money in people's pockets, you'll get a good response. *All* of us wanted raises. Some people out there might look at a $5,741 raise and say's that it's no big deal—but being a single mother, and a woman of color, that raise was huge because I'm constantly broke."

The point here is not that racial divisions in public education have been overcome, nor that strategies to build working-class unity should ignore race. Such claims would be absurd in a country where the legacy of Native American genocide, chattel slavery, and Jim Crow continues to profoundly structure politics and society. As Price notes, the strikes did not automatically reveal these underlying dynamics to her white coworkers: "The raise we got was a big win, and there was a lot of unity in the walkout. But it's not as if most teachers here have now started digging deeper into the realities of structural racism."

In Kentucky, tensions over broader questions of institutionalized oppression proved to be especially problematic. In April, the walkout movement's interracial unity began to fray after neither the Kentucky Education Association nor the rank-and-file network KY United We Stand agreed to the

---

10   Cole Hargrave Snodgrass & Associates, *A Survey of 5,487 Holding Oklahoma Teaching Certifications but Not Currently Teaching in Oklahoma Public Schools under the Age of 65*, Oklahoma City: Oklahoma State Department of Education, September–October 2017, sde.ok.gov.

proposal of a group of Black teachers and white allies in Louisville to include demands against an impending racist "gang bill," HB 169.

Even in those places where movement leadership was most actively focused on overcoming racial divisions—like Arizona—significant gaps remained. This was especially the case when it came to building unity with school support staff, who in Arizona tend to be disproportionately Spanish speakers. Teacher leader Dylan Wegela explains the challenges: "Support staff definitely *did* participate in the movement, [and] we did try to translate as much of the material, and the discussion, as possible—but it wasn't always easy to get it done."

Whatever the strengths and limitations of such unitary emphasis, in the West Virginia, Oklahoma, and Arizona strikes it proved to be crucial in coalescing workers from a wide range of backgrounds and ideological persuasions. Without it, it's hard to imagine the participation of individuals like the Arizonan striker who posted this message on the first day of the walkout: "I am conservative. I am Catholic. I am a public school teacher. I am walking and prepared for the long haul . . . until whenever." A unitary approach was also key to involving those who considered themselves generally uninterested in politics, like the following teacher from Arizona: "I learned that true power comes from such a vast group of people setting aside their individual stories to become part of a larger voice. I've never been comfortable with politics, but when you believe in something as much as Red for Ed, you have got to do something."

It was through experiences similar to these that thousands of conservative educators began to question their Republican affinities. A redirection of popular anger upward, against the ruling rich, has profound anti-racist implications. Though the process is uneven and far from automatic, scapegoating marginalized groups tends to lose its political traction when a viable class-based alternative is presented. Consider the reflections of one white teacher following the strike: "I'm an Arizona native and please forgive me for being asleep my entire life . . . Red for Ed has awoken my spirit of justice, truth, love, and respect for all people. I will not return to my previous slumber but fight for the many with little against the few with much."

One of the fundamental reasons why the movement's emphasis on unity proved so effective was that its demands were not merely limited to those of teachers. In addition to a consistent emphasis on student needs, the walkouts in all three states were of and for *all* school employees, including bus drivers, custodians, secretaries, cooks, and paraprofessionals. The role of support staff workers was absolutely central, though the extent to which each strike overcame the teacher–staff divide varied significantly.

Unlike divisions of ideology, union membership, or willingness to strike, the relationship between teachers and other school employees is a distinctly structural and hierarchical one. At most schools, support staff receive the least respect, the fewest benefits, and the lowest wages; many make less than half the pay of teachers. As one bus driver posted on Facebook: "I am constantly being reminded that, 'I need to be professional' by my superiors. Perhaps that argument would carry more clout if my wages reflected that of a professional . . . #justsayin." In this context, the challenge of overcoming the isolation of support staff parallels the more often discussed difficulties of overcoming racial and gender divisions within the working class.

Within the education system, support staff are often overlooked. Many people I spoke with felt that this was the deepest divide among school employees. Linda Vanuss, a cafeteria cook in Ravenswood, West Virginia, explained: "I love my job, but we really don't feel like we are part of the school. For instance, they have faculty dinners that we're not invited to and that they then ask us to do the dishes for." Head custodian Pam Shamblin made a similar point about the previous school she worked at: "I was treated like dirt."

Seeing the need to build the widest possible unity, rank-and-file leaders in West Virginia and Arizona consciously sought to build a movement that extended beyond just teachers. The names of their groups—West Virginia Public Employees United and Arizona Educators United—were not accidental. As the latter explained in its online FAQ: "So many different job families are involved in the day to day operations of our public schools, that we just say 'educators.'" Moreover, both groups consciously pushed for demands that would unify all school employees. "You need to organize people around a specific issue," noted Jay O'Neal. "For us, it was the insurance. That's a big-tent issue that affected one in seven West Virginians."

Organizers in Arizona took a similarly expansive approach. When Governor Ducey promised a 20 percent *teacher* pay raise to head off the impending strike, Red for Ed leaders didn't take the bait. At their press conference explaining the reasons why they were rejecting the deal, Phoenix school-staff representative Vanessa Jimenez noted, "[Ducey] made no mention of education support professionals. So that saddens me because everybody knows that it takes a village to raise our students—and that village includes teachers and classified staff . . . When I think of his proposal, it's clearly an attempt to divide us. We're not going to be divided. We're in this together."

Stressing the contributions and dignity of the tens of thousands of service personnel was necessary to undercut the tendency of the media—as well as many rank-and-file teachers—to justify the protests by arguing that teacher pay was too low given their high educational levels and their specific professional responsibilities. Against such narrow framing, Pam Shamblin in Ravenswood insisted that "this was a labor movement for *everyone*, not just teachers."

Unfortunately, support staff marginalization within the schools and the movement did not disappear overnight. As is so often the case, the stratification of working people made it difficult for workers to recognize the particular plight of their worse-off peers. Given this challenging context, it took sustained efforts by militant support staff in West Virginia to prevent their coworkers from standing aside from the general struggle. Mary Wykle—a bus driver in Wyoming County who played a key role in mobilizing other service personnel—explains: "Many of us felt left out because everybody kept calling this a teachers' movement, a teachers' strike. I understood why personnel often got discouraged by this—but it was counterproductive. So I ended up giving pep talks to them, to explain why we all needed to be in this struggle together."

These efforts paid off. Unlike in the 1990 West Virginia teachers' strike—when schools remained open through the labor of support staff and scabs—this time all employees went out together. Linda Vanuss recalls the ensuing transformation at her school: "We're usually ignored, but during the strike it was different—we were united. I felt like when teachers looked at me, they saw me more like an equal."

The capacity of West Virginia support staff to sustain their participation in the walkout was also aided greatly by the initiative of Cathy Kunkel and Stephen Smith—leftist organizer allies of O'Neal and Comer in Charleston—to launch a GoFundMe strike fund. Through small donations from across the country, the initiative raised $332,945—roughly half of which went to school support staff and substitute teachers. Whereas full-time teachers got paid during the strike because superintendents canceled school, the same was not true for other personnel like unsalaried support staff, teachers' aides, and substitutes, many of whom live paycheck to paycheck.

Without the efforts of service personnel, victory would have remained elusive. In the words of Emily Comer: "There's been a common misconception that we won because we had the support of superintendents. But, really, we were able to win because we were able to shut the schools down. And we were only able to do that because we had everyone on board—custodians, cooks, bus drivers, teachers' aides. Schools cannot run without them."

This dynamic became clear on Wednesday, February 28, the pivotal "cooling-off day" after West Virginia's governor and union leaders ordered workers to return to work on Thursday. As educators across the state debated if and how to defy this edict, support staff took the initiative to make it clear to superintendents—and teachers—that they were staying out. When bus drivers at mass meetings in Charleston and in southern counties announced that "the buses will not run tomorrow," they received standing ovations. By all accounts, the initiatives of drivers like Mary Wykle in Wyoming County to prepare for hard picket lines were pivotal in the ultimate decision of superintendents across the state that evening: schools would remain shut. "The service personnel were our saving grace," notes Nicole McCormick. "In Mercer County, some schools would have gone back on Thursday, but they couldn't open without their bus drivers and cooks."

In Oklahoma, support staff participation was much lower—in fact, most continued to report to work throughout the walkout, even when there were no classes in session. This development, which significantly weakened the impact of Oklahoma's work stoppage, was rooted in various sources. Though inspired by Mountain State strikers, the inexperienced rank-and-file groups that sprung up in Oklahoma did not consistently assimilate all of West Virginia's lessons.

Unlike in the other states, they did not establish a strike fund for those in need. The names of the Sooner State's Facebook group—Oklahoma Teachers United and Oklahoma Teacher Walkout: The Time Is Now—were also indicative of a somewhat narrower approach.

This generalized inability to incorporate service personnel into the work stoppage was above all the result of a broader limitation of Oklahoma's strike: teachers in the Sooner State could legally miss work and receive pay if their superintendents voluntarily canceled school, but the same was not true for service personnel. For this reason, to quote Amanda Ewing, Associate Executive Director of the Oklahoma Education Association, "Though they tried to support the movement in their districts, it was rare for support staff to attend the protests at the capitol; most ended up reporting to work each day."

Oklahoma's limited staff participation in the walkout illustrates an important point: the fight for working-class unity is always inseparable from broader political questions—in this case, a willingness to challenge superintendents and potentially break the law. While it's relatively easy to affirm the need for unity, actually building a united movement is easier said than done.

Community Support

Labor law in the United States is uniquely structured to divide working people. By prohibiting most public and private sector workers from bargaining over issues relevant to broader layers of the working class, the American state succeeded in narrowing organized labor's purview to the economic demands of its members alone. This, in turn, led much of the nonunionized working class to treat "Big Labor" as just another special interest group looking out for itself.

In 1995, faced with steady marginalization and decline, the AFL-CIO officially adopted a strategic orientation toward winning public support through broader community alliances. This was a significant step forward from the narrow business unionism of years prior. Yet labor's continuing crisis over the following two decades showed that this strategy was no political panacea. The devil, as they say, is in the details.

For most unions, building unity with the community has meant working with liberal nonprofits to promote electoral campaigns or, at best, to organize demonstrations in support of progressive demands. Much of this work is laudable. But, as critics like Jane McAlevey and Joe Burns have pointed out, labor's current social justice approach suffers from two critical flaws. First, it has gone hand in hand with an abandonment of the strike weapon. Second, this approach has depended on alliances from on high—with relatively weak nonprofits and community leaders—instead of relying on rank-and-file workers to organize and mobilize the broader working-class communities of which they are an integral part.

However, a different model of social justice unionism exists—one capable of generating the power required to win. By leaning on the leverage of workplace militancy, raising demands on behalf of the whole working class, and tapping into strikers' deep social networks, the red state revolt showed what this alternative looks like in practice.

From day one, educators were well aware of the necessity to gain, and hold on to, community support. Indeed, much of the initial opposition to a strike came from educators' fears that the public would turn on them if they walked out on students. To win parent and student support, teachers in West Virginia, like Arizona, began grassroots organizing months before they voted to go on strike. They took every opportunity for discussion with parents, explaining that educator working conditions were students' learning conditions. They waved signs, passed out informational fliers, and organized morning "walk-ins," during which they rallied together with parents and students alike.

As the walkouts approached, educators began collecting food donations to give to those large numbers of children who were dependent on school lunches and free breakfasts. Once the strikes began, teachers spent untold volunteer hours collecting and distributing food to these same students, often hand-delivering care packages to their homes.

One of the strikers' secrets to success was that they consistently raised political demands—for example, massively increased school funding—that lay outside the restricted bounds of normal collective bargaining. The defense of student interests was consistently placed front and center. At a press conference announcing their impending work stoppage, Noah Karvelis explained: "We are underfunding our students every single day—every single student in the state of Arizona is being underfunded. And by doing so we are throwing away an entire generation's opportunity for academic success." And in Oklahoma, the work stoppage focused almost exclusively on demands for increased school funding, since the legislature had already passed important salary concessions in a last-minute attempt to prevent educators from walking out.

Fighting for students, and framing their struggles as a defense of essential services for the public, went a long way toward undercutting the Right's constant harping that striking teachers were hurting children. Educators made a compelling case that they weren't walking from the students, but *for* them. As one West Virginia teacher explained in a March 1 letter to her students: "I love you and that's why I'm doing this." Posts from Arizonan strikers conveyed a similar message: "I educated my students the best way I know how, and that's by taking that stand and showing them that they're worth that time and effort. If we can get them to believe they're worth us walking out then maybe they can be our loudest advocates."

Students reciprocated this support by taking matters into their own hands. During each of the strikes, high schoolers organized massive rallies in defense of their teachers and public education. As Tucson high school student Patrick Robles declared on April 23, "My teachers have stood for me, and now I will stand for them on the picket line."

Together with her classmate Juliana Purdue, Jazmine Aliff of Seth, West Virginia, made a last-minute Facebook event in hopes of getting a hundred students to demonstrate their solidarity. "The reason we did it was simple," she told me. "Our teachers do so much for us and we know that a lot of them felt down during the strike, like they were failing us by not being in class. We wanted to show that we supported them—and we wanted to fire them back up." To the organizers' surprise, over 2,500 students joined the rally.

Another crucial ingredient of striking educators' mass appeal was their contestation of the Right's attempts to pit them against other working people in the state. Like their counterparts in West Virginia and Oklahoma, Red for Ed leaders sharply opposed Republican maneuvers to increase public education funding through cuts to vital social programs. Against Governor Ducey's proposal to give teachers a raise off the backs of other services, union vice president Marisol Garcia made this point clear: "They're going to rob money from the developmentally disabled? They're going to take money from the arts? They're going to sweep money from Medicaid? That's not what teachers want to see from the future. They want real revenue streams brought into Arizona."

The experience of these strikes—like the Sanders campaign of 2016—revealed that even in deep-red states, there is a majoritarian basis for independent working-class politics. And, contrary to the hopes of Republicans and the initial fears of educators, public support actually *increased* after the strikes began. A week into the walkout in Oklahoma, for instance, polls found that 72 percent of the state now supported the continuation of the educators' strike "until all of their demands are met." Similar developments took place nationwide, and one poll found that of those Americans who had heard of the strikes, 80 percent approved of them.[11] There's an important lesson here: public opinion is fluid, and it can shift in the direction of workers, provided they take a stand. Rather than moderating one's politics to accommodate a mythical center, the only way to truly test the potentialities of popular support is through systematic organizing and the process of mass action itself.

Unlike numerous teachers' struggles in US history, most notably the 1968 New York City strike, the 2018 actions received strong backing from African American and Latino parents. By foregrounding demands on behalf of students, the walkouts also took important strides toward bridging existing racial divides. In each of these states, the student body was disproportionately made up of people of color; and in Arizona the majority of students were nonwhite.

Demands for increased school funding were particularly popular among Black and Brown working-class families, for whom austerity has had an especially devastating impact. To quote Stephanie Price of Oklahoma: "I never saw an instance where parents from communities of color didn't support the struggle." Indeed, the "race-blind" demand for more school funds was objectively anti-racist insofar as it would have disproportionately benefited these families. "Districts in Arizona with high Hispanic populations definitely generally supported education more," notes Dylan Wegela.

---

11 Alexia Fernández Campbell, "Most Republicans and Democrats Agree That American Teachers Need a Raise," *Vox*, April 24, 2018, vox. com.

Arizona's walkout was a particularly remarkable example of multiracial working-class solidarity. The state has a vicious recent history of anti-immigrant xenophobia, and Latinos are the largest group of students in the school system. Unsurprisingly, the same Koch-funded forces pushing school privatization are also open advocates of the anti-immigrant border wall and stepped-up ICE deportations. By channeling working people's anger into a broad struggle for common demands, the strike provided a clear alternative to right-wing racism. Organizers consciously sought to make the movement as inclusive as possible to all educators and parents. All official Red For Ed placards, for instance, were printed in English on one side and Spanish on the other—not a minor detail in a state where the politics of language has long been central to the right-wing agenda.

AEU leader Vanessa Arredondo-Aguirre played a particularly central role in these activities, creating a specific AEU Facebook page in Spanish for Latino parents and school employees, and coordinating much of the media outreach to Spanish-language stations. "I'd do interviews for Telemundo and Univision," she recalls, "and my message would always be the same: 'We're fighting for your kids.'" These publicity efforts paid off. As one Latino parent posted on Facebook: "Got more information from Mexican stations than from American stations. They were up to date on all points. Very supporting!"

Still, Arredondo-Aguirre insists that in-person conversations were the most important: "The community where I live, it's a border town, so a lot of teachers went out talking

to people door to door, we went with fliers in Spanish informing them about Red for Ed and our demands. In my experience, I'd say that about 90 percent of responses were positive—we had a lot of support."

The experience of the spring 2018 strikes showed that
there's no zero-sum relationship between broad working-
class movements and fights against racial injustice. Rather,
workplace organizing, at its best, can serve as *the* strategic
anchor for fighting all forms of oppression. For example,
Arizona's Red for Ed movement, while concentrating on
education-specific demands, also helped generate political
space and a broader audience for the fight for immigrants'
rights.

At a June 30 rally against President Trump's family sepa-
rations, Red for Ed leader Derek Harris livestreamed the
following message to their Facebook group: "I know it's not
our core issue, but it *is* an important issue because we're
doing this for our friends, our families, our students. We're
doing all of our [Red for Ed] things for the kids and we get
immigrant families that come in, we teach them too, and we
want them to have as good an education as anybody else.
Sometimes they're traumatized by the events getting here or
after they arrive. Our kids are counting on us in so many
ways—so stand for them in every way you can."

Parents and community members of all backgrounds
returned their support for educators in a myriad of ways.
Simple actions—like honking while driving by an informational picket line, or thanking a teacher at the grocery store—
were significant morale boosts. Frequently, community

members also brought water and donuts to the picket line or picked up the tab for strikers at restaurants.

A big strike is made up of many small acts of solidarity. One highlight was the unexpected encouragement educators received from parents. In my conversations with teachers, many recounted experiences similar to that of Tanya Asleson in Ravenswood. While delivering food on the day West Virginia educators decided to go wildcat, she expected resistance from parents: "I went to the house of a parent who was really poor, his kids always desperately need food at school. The strike was a real hardship for his family—but instead of telling me to go back to work, he said: 'M'aam, you stay strong now. You haven't won yet, don't go back tomorrow.' It was *so* moving."

A number of local institutions also lent their support to the strikers. Contingents of unionized workers from other industrial sectors were a common sight at the big rallies; many issued public messages of solidarity and donated food and water to the educators. Most importantly, unionized construction workers at the capitol in Oklahoma refused to cross the picket line, halting the building's $200 million retrofit. And though the AFL-CIO, National Education Association (NEA), and AFT unfortunately failed to organize any systematic national support campaign, solidarity messages and photos from individual unions across the country similarly bolstered the educators' spirits.

Churches proved to be no less politically important. Once the strikes began, a large number of church buildings became makeshift childcare sites and food distribution centers. Rank-and-file workers and their family members also brought the movement directly to their co-religionists. As one Arizona teacher explained on April 22, "I just talked to my 94-year-old mother who proudly told me that she had worn Red for Ed to church and to her women's group meeting and had talked to everyone she could about our cause. Oh, and we are also on the prayer list. #churchladieshaveourback."

Given pervasive liberal stereotypes about bible-thumpers in Trumpland, it should be underlined that religious beliefs were not an obstacle to active participation in class struggle. In fact, during the strikes widespread religious sentiment generally helped promote and sustain mass action in the face of considerable adversity. Strikers on Facebook frequently reminded their peers that "God helps those who help themselves," and that it was necessary to "put legs on our prayers." Jennifer Deibel's "#RedForEd PRAY-in" conveyed the general sentiment: "As you continue to walk-in, wear red, contact your representatives and fight for what's best for Arizona students, would you commit to taking a few moments each day to hit your knees and fight in prayer." On Monday, March 5, thousands of West Virginian educators participated in a powerful joint prayer inside the capitol rotunda. "Now that is how you strike. Beautiful!" replied one educator on the United page.

Though national celebrities were noticeably absent, some important local figures lent their support. For instance, Oklahoma State's head football coach Mike Gundy, one of the most beloved individuals in the state, took a clear stand on the side of the walkout: "I'm 100 percent behind our educators . . . and I think they should do whatever they think is necessary in order to get what's necessary to be successful."[12]

Local Democratic leaders also came out in support of the educators, playing a significant role in legitimizing their demands. For some, this attitude clearly stemmed from personal conviction. But for most Democratic representatives, particularly in the higher echelons of the party, electoral calculations seem to have been the overriding factor. Sensing that these movements could be their ticket back to power, politicians had nothing to lose by jumping on the strikers' bandwagon. In the words of Emily Comer: "If workers hadn't taken the lead, the Democrats would never have taken the stand that they did."

National solidarity efforts were also critically important in bolstering the strikers. Educators, teachers' unions, and supportive socialists from across the country wore red to work and took photos of themselves with messages of support. "People might think these solidarity photos were no big deal, but actually they were hugely important to us," explained Jay O'Neal. "Being on strike is really physically draining, and these small acts gave us strength to keep fighting." In a message of encouragement to public employees, Emily Comer posted the following note on March 3: "We are inspiring the entire nation! We're leading the way for other

---

12   "OSU Coach Mike Gundy: 'I'm 100 percent behind our educators'," April 5, 2018, koco.com

workers who have been ignored for too long and they're watching us for guidance."

Pizza donations were another emblematic crystallization of national support. The tradition began when my mother, Lita Blanc, president of the United Educators of San Francisco, ordered hundreds of pizzas for striking West Virginia educators during the last two days of their strike. A GoFundMe page comment described the morale boost when the food arrived: "I was at the Capitol yesterday when pizzas were delivered inside. It was like pizza crowd surfing!!! Pizza boxes were floating across hands of teachers up in the air. After the pizza was gone, the boxes made great drums for the chanting! Lol. Again, thank you from the bottom of my heart!"

Among conservatives, views of blue states even began to shift, as seen in the following note sent to the SF educators' union by a Mountain State striker: "Thank you for your support of West Virginia teachers. People of California get a lot of bad press. Obviously, it isn't fair for all of you."

Empowerment and Politicization

Concessions wrested from employers are not the only manifest impact of strikes. Equally important, work stoppages also empower and politicize the working class. One Arizona educator posted on Facebook that, "During the walkout I felt more empowered and respected as a teacher than ever before. We all get the 'I'm so sorry' looks when we say we are teachers. I never experienced that once. I was suddenly an activist and hero."

Strikes constitute a dramatic break from normal routines and social hierarchies. At most times and places, workers under capitalism have remarkably little say over their jobs, communities, or government. Even if workers are allowed to vote periodically, it is unaccountable employers and the politicians at their service who possess systemic decision-making power over economic and political life. Mostly, working people just try to keep their heads down and get by.

Before these movements began, labor organizations in West Virginia, Oklahoma, and Arizona were numerically weak and/or hollowed out. Most educators who joined the unions did so primarily to receive legal services in case of disciplinary conflicts. WVEA regional organizer Allen Stumps described the situation in West Virginia, where the unions were relatively strong in comparison with Oklahoma and Arizona: "Prior to the push for a strike, it was very tough to organize. We'd be happy if ten people would show up to a meeting."

All this changed dramatically over the course of the strikes. A groundswell of collective action went hand in hand with an unprecedented union membership surge. The influx of thousands of new members decisively vindicated those dissident labor militants and analysts who for years have been arguing that reviving the strike was *the* key to labor revitalization. It's hard to imagine how educators will be able to sustain their power and win further gains in the coming period without this continued revival of organized labor; indeed, while Facebook can be a valuable tool during moments of peak mobilization, there's no strategic substitute for a strong trade union movement.

And membership increases only tell part of the story, for there were many union members who did not become active until this movement emerged. Tanya Asleson's experience was not atypical: "I went from not wanting to be a building rep, to being aggravated and involved, to now becoming president of the AFT in our county. The strike forced me to find leadership skills within myself. We've all really grown in the last couple of months; it makes us proud."

To be sure, much of this organizational and leadership development took place outside formal union structures. To quote Katie Endicott: "We learned that you don't have to have a union title, a position. You just have to have courage and a backbone to stand up for yourself, for your state, and your kids. And that's what we did." In Arizona, in fact, self-organized ranks directly led the strike. Arizona Educators United, formed in early March, immediately developed a volunteer site-liaison network of 2,000 school-based organizer-representatives, the overwhelming majority of whom had no prior activist experience. When asked to describe their highlight of the walkout, one Arizonan educator posted the following: "Saying Yes to being a liaison – not my personality! Huge personal growth!"

Referring to the strikes as "endurance tests," teachers emphasized the challenges of staying out for so long—and how easy it was to fall into despair along the way. "The longer it went, the more it felt like we weren't going to win our demands," recalls Mingo County teacher Eric Starr. "It was like trench warfare—and it seemed like the Senate was out to bust the union. The longer it went on, the more stressed I became, but I didn't want to go back to school and tell the students that I had folded." Even for educators used to a demanding job, physical exhaustion was a very real problem. According to Tanya Asleson, "By the end of the strike I felt like I needed to go back to work to get some rest."

One reason for this exhaustion was the intensity of the capitol actions. Due to the noise and crowd numbers, these often felt like outdoor music festivals or playoff sporting events—except with much higher stakes. In Oklahoma, there was all-day picketing, lobbying, and dancing, punctuated by noontime rallies. Political discussion was incessant among the educators camped out in front of the building. All throughout the day, educators proudly carried their home-made protest signs and admired those of their peers.

Midway through the Sooner State's walkout, Stephanie Price described the scene: "Being at the capitol is empowering and exhausting. It's crowded and chaotic; it also often means waiting for hours in line to get inside the capitol. But at the same time, it's so positive and emotional, people have been really polite and kind to each other. People are coming together to find a solution to a common goal. It feels good."

The capitol protest in Phoenix was very similar, although it was marked by intense heat and outfitted with an even better marching band. One Arizona educator posted that her favorite part of the strike was "getting a teacher who I never thought would participate down to the capitol." The only downside, she noted, was that now she couldn't get "[Twisted Sister's] 'We're not Gonna Take It' out of [her] head."

West Virginia's protest, in contrast, was relatively no frills. There were no daily rallies, no sound system, and no campout infrastructure. Each day the protest consisted almost entirely of chanting and singing in front of the Senate chamber doors. It's significant that protestors at the West Virginia capitol never sang labor songs—instead, anthems like John Denver's "Country Roads" or the White Stripes' "Seven Nation Army" were the norm. Though one could certainly find many teachers decked out in traditional red bandannas, the strike's level of political-cultural continuity with West Virginia's militant past was lower than portrayed in most outside accounts. Protest signs were far more likely to reference Beyoncé than Mother Jones.

When I asked West Virginia educators to describe a particular moment when they had gained a newfound sense of power, many cited the numerous confrontations between teachers and leading Republicans. Such in-person clashes played an important role in unmasking the politicians' veneer of legitimacy and in giving educators confidence in themselves. Ashlea Bassham's anecdote was typical:

My favorite moment of the strike was on the second day. Me and seven of my coworkers were waiting in a hallway where we hoped we'd be able to corner Senator Karnes, the vice chair of the Education Committee—and a real reactionary. Eventually, Karnes comes out and we start asking him things like "Why are you being anti-teacher?" He responded in this really arrogant way, interrupting us and telling us made-up things like that our average class size was fifteen.

Eventually my coworker goes up to him and says "Why do you keep talking over people? It seems like that's the one thing you're good at." Keep in mind that my coworker is *not* an outspoken guy and he's generally very polite. So I really wasn't expecting him to speak up; it was great to see that bit of empowerment. It felt like we were finally starting to stand up to the bullies who run our state.

For most educators I spoke with, the single most empowering moment of the strike was the night it went wildcat. On the cold evening of Tuesday, February 27, thousands of striking educators gathered on the outside steps of the capitol, having heard that union leaders were meeting with the governor and that the national press would be filming live at six. WVEA president Dale Lee and AFT-WV president Christine Campbell strode to the top of the steps and quieted the restless crowd. Only ten minutes earlier, everybody's phones had begun buzzing with the announcement of the deal's details at the governor's last-minute press conference inside the capitol. Strikers were incensed when they saw that the deal fell decidedly short of their expectations.

In an epic misreading of the situation, Dale Lee calmly announced to the massive crowd that the strike was over, and that they would return to work on Thursday. The ensuing confrontation was perhaps the defining moment of the entire strike wave. As he tried to finish his declaration, Lee clearly didn't know what had hit him:

We're going back in Thursday, but we reserve the right [growing boos] . . . Hold up, hold up, hold up [Lee raises his hand to quiet the crowd], hold up please. [From the crowd: "No you please hold up!"]. We reserve the right to call you back out as we need to [Loud shouts: "No! Boo!"]

Drowning out Christine Campbell's subsequent attempt to speak, the crowd of educators began chanting, "55 united! 55 united!," "Fix it now! Fix it now!," "Back to the table! Back to the table!," and "We are the union bosses! We are the union bosses!"

Rank-and-file leader Jay O'Neal was one of the many teachers assembled that night. He later explained to me: "It was my favorite moment of the whole strike. I was watching everyone around me and my jaw dropped. I saw that people, my coworkers who had felt powerless for so long, now after four days of striking felt their collective power. When they yelled 'We are the union bosses!' they really meant it. It was so beautiful to witness that realization."

Everybody now acknowledges that the wildcat saved the strike. Contrary to the message of the unions and the governor that evening, the Republican West Virginia Senate had *not* in fact agreed to a deal. Had school employees ceded to their union leaders' command to return to work on Thursday, they may well have won nothing.

It took another full week of striking to make the Senate back down. In the late morning of Tuesday, March 6, Governor Jim Justice waded into the crowd rallying inside the capitol and announced, to the surprise of all, that the

Republican Senate had finally agreed to the strikers' demands. Once it became clear that this deal was indeed final, the capitol was immediately engulfed with celebration. Strikers broke down crying, hugged friends and strangers, sang songs, and chanted as loudly as they could.

Immediately following the announcement, Emily Comer described the scene to me: "We're overwhelmed with emotion. I have broken down sobbing more times than I can count today. There's probably video footage of me bawling while I'm surrounded by coworkers singing 'Country Roads.' There's almost a sense of disbelief, because for about a solid week there, we were really in unfamiliar territory."

Jay O'Neal conveyed a similar sentiment: "I'm excited, I'm thrilled, I feel like my life won't ever be the same again. It sounds like hyperbole, but it's not. Going back to the classroom won't be the same now."

The strikers' final chant in the capitol was fitting: "*Who* made history? *We* made history!"

Arizona's victory came in the predawn hours of May 3. To ensure that the pay-raise deal passed—and to support the fight to add progressive amendments to it—AEU leaders had called upon strikers the afternoon prior to remain on the capitol grounds. That evening's all-night campout was a highlight for many, ranking with the 75,000-strong march that had kicked off the strike a week before. Thousands participated in a candlelight vigil, capped by a group rendition of "Amazing Grace." As one educator recalled on the Facebook group, "It gave me goosebumps and when I tried to tell my mom about it today, I started crying." There was something in the air. As teachers camped out on the capitol grounds, the ever-popular marching band led an ongoing nighttime sing-along (punctuated only by periodic pizza breaks).

People were reluctant to leave, even after the capitol lawn's sprinklers came on. All the while, hundreds of red-clad educators packed into the legislative chambers, remaining there well past 3:00 a.m. One can glean a sense of the crowd's irreverent mood from the following Twitter request: "Can someone please bring a pizza up to 3rd floor of the Senate? They won't let us back up if [we] go down. And also a Coke??? #redneedsfed #kiddingnotkidding #maybejust-thecoke #notthatkoch #caffeinatemeplease." The request was quickly met.

When the budget deal was finally passed in the early morning hours, educators were celebratory, although somewhat less euphoric than in West Virginia, because they had not yet won their demands for full school funding. Despite having gotten only a few hours of sleep, thousands nevertheless returned to the capitol later that morning for a lively mass rally to celebrate their achievements. A teacher's freshly made sign put it well: "Best group project ever."

The return to work was no less emotional. As one Wyoming County, West Virginia teacher remarked, "I've never been hugged so much in my life." Educators posted hundreds of moving anecdotes on social media about their first day back at school. One of Vanessa Arredondo-Aguirre's third graders gave her the following card, replete with Wonder Woman stickers: "Thank you for all your courage

Ms. Arredondo. You are my hero." That same day, another Arizona teacher posted the following to the AEU page: "I just had a student come up to me and say thanks for fighting for me coach. That made all of the struggles and sacrifices worth while."

Pride was a common theme of teachers after these victories, just as it had been throughout the strike. "My feelings about West Virginia have changed a lot. Before this, I felt politically isolated and was ready to leave the state, but the unity has really affected me," noted Azareen Mullins. "The biggest change in me since we won is the deep pride I feel in the people of this state and our accomplishment. I've seen that not everyone is asleep at the wheel, that there are other people here willing to fight."

These processes of empowerment went along with a rapid and deep politicization of tens of thousands of workers, students, and parents. For weeks on end, politics became the 24/7 topic of conservation. Asleson recalls that "during those nine days of striking, when I wasn't at the capitol or our picket line, I was glued to my phone, checking for updates and watching the capitol's livestream. I couldn't even bring myself to watch a movie." The West Virginia legislature website repeatedly crashed due to network overload.

When you're involved in collective action, it no longer makes sense to tune out politics. Whereas liberals and academics tend to treat education as a precondition for progressive action, the red state revolts demonstrate the actuality of an old socialist axiom: most working-class people learn about social power through their experiences in struggle and mass organizing. A book or a lecture cannot effectively explain, on a mass scale, ideas like solidarity or collective action; for these to sink in, you need to experience them firsthand.

Given the diversity of strike participants and community supporters, this politicization has, of course, proceeded unevenly. These strikes were only the initial shots in a much-longer battle through which working people can come to realize the depth of their power, differentiate political friend from foe, and see the possibility for a radically better society.

But even in the span of just a few short months, some basic lessons in class consciousness reverberated widely. The importance of trade unions and worker solidarity became widely evident. So too did the potency of the strike weapon. In the words of Noah Karvelis: "Educators saw that they have power. They've realized that they're exploited and that they have structural power. And in this walkout, they made their power felt." For Emily Comer, "more than anything, the strike changed people's ideas of what is possible. I now have coworkers asking me about when we're going to have a nationwide teachers' strike, which I could have never imagined being uttered even a few months ago."

Among educators' takeaways from the strikes, disillusionment with Republican politicians was a common theme. Facebook feeds were flooded by Republican educators repenting their past ballot decisions and denouncing their current leaders. On March 5, a West Virginia teacher repented: "I won't ever vote for another Republican in this state again." To this, another replied: "My mom is a Republican and at this time I wouldn't vote for her."

Strikers in Oklahoma and Arizona put forward similar critiques. To quote one post:

> Conservative, Christian, Republican and I support RedforEd. I'm astonished and mortified that Republicans leaders are undermining education so callously. I believe in families and that children are blessings. I cannot understand why the idea of increasing funding for education is not their top priority. If you want to say you are for protecting families, you have to fund education accordingly.

Such sentiments did not just remain on paper. Unlike their private sector counterparts, public employees have the opportunity to vote out their bosses, and so in the wake of the strikes, hundreds of educators decided to run for office to challenge anti-education Republicans in Oklahoma, West Virginia, and Arizona. The basic political intuition behind this electoral surge is correct: protests aren't enough. Indeed, systematic transformation of the priorities of a state—or the country—requires political power. Given this fact, and the role played by local Democrats during the strike, it is not surprising that many teachers and staff in these states enthusiastically voted to kick out local Republicans in November 2018.

The problem, however, is that the Democratic Party is not a party of, or for, the working class; in fact, elected Democrats have a long tradition of pro-business policies and broken promises in each of these states. Through their experience in struggle, a layer of teachers in the spring of 2018 concluded that it was necessary to act independently of either party. The strikes, after all, demonstrated that mass struggle can win major gains no matter *who* is in power. As one rank-and-file teacher commented in the AEU group: "I've also come to realize just how deep the problems in government are. I know everyone keeps saying we need to vote in Democrats, but that's not the answer. Educational funding problems exist in highly Democratic states too." A post on West Virginia's United page voiced similar sentiments: "I'm not the far left and not the far right. This is what WV Democrats used to be before this total demise of our party. Maybe we should start a 3rd party."

The extent of the subordination of politicians and governmental policy to big business was a key revelation for many strikers. According to one West Virginia teacher: "What I did gain from the strike was knowledge . . . and what I learned scares me. I learned that most of our legislators do not respect our profession. I learned that most of them are not willing to help the working class because it conflicts with their loyalties to the gas/oil industry or pharmaceutical companies."

At Oklahoma's student rally during the walkout, sixteen-year-old Cameron Olbert reached a similar conclusion: "The poor and working class . . . have already paid more than enough into the system. It's time to ask those who can best afford it to pay their fair share too. That means we stop starving public education just so we can feed Big Oil."

Opposition to privatization spread widely, particularly in Arizona. Parent activist Dawn Penich-Thacker explained the dynamic: "Red for Ed has more people paying attention to education than ever before. Even last year, a lot of people hadn't heard of the funding crisis, let alone vouchers. Now you can't go anywhere in Arizona without talking about this. Red for Ed is an incredible 'force multiplier' for efforts to put a stop to increased privatization: it makes all of our tools more powerful. Now every conversation we have about vouchers and charters is amplified across the state."

Though the initial demands of these education movements may seem relatively modest, each walkout raised a question with radical political implications: Should our society's wealth and resources be used for human needs, or for corporate profits? A small, but not insignificant, number of strikers concluded that systematic solutions will be needed to resolve our society's underlying crisis of priorities. In this sense, it's fitting to end our chapter with a letter sent to me by Morgantown teacher Anna Simmons. When asked about her favorite moment of the strike, she recounted the following anecdote from the day West Virginian educators went wildcat:

> At a mostly unoccupied mall in Morgantown we met to discuss our options. Ultimately, in a nearly singular voice, we stated that we were not willing to accept the same empty promises our politicians have given their constituents for decades. It was a spontaneously planned meeting with short notice but our school employees showed up in huge numbers.
>
> I realized that night that I wasn't the only one feeling as passionately as I was feeling about what the work

stoppage meant. It was the moment I realized that it was about more than just insurance premiums and salaries. It was the continuation of a movement that started with Bernie Sanders and is going to result in a power shift from the elite wealthy to the working people.

3
THE MILITANT MINORITY

"Something was coming to a head, but it didn't have to be a strike—and especially not a strike that *won*."

—West Virginia teacher Nicole McCormick

According to most national media accounts, the red state revolt was a spontaneous upsurge. Conditions were bad and teachers rose up en masse—end of story.

It's true that these strikes were marked by an extraordinarily high level of self-activity outside formal organizational structures. Much of the struggle developed independently of any conscious interventions by experienced activists. But these strike movements were not completely leaderless, nor purely spontaneous. In fact, it's impossible to separate their course from the efforts of those rank-and-file organizers that helped spark and guide them, in alliance—and sometimes in conflict—with the top trade union leadership. The point is not simply that some individual or group always has to take the initiative in mass struggle. Rather, it was the specific political perspectives and tactical choices of a dedicated core of militant teachers that most decisively shaped these strikes' dynamics and outcomes.

To be sure, these grassroots activists did not conjure a mass movement out of thin air. As shown in the preceding chapters, a whole series of economic and political processes underlay the upsurge. And unions, with all their contradictions, played a pivotal role in coordinating and strengthening these movements. Yet, had it not been for the efforts of such rank-and-file organizers, things could have turned out very differently. Without activist interventions, for instance, it's unlikely that rank and filers would have been able to overcome the hesitations of their top union leadership. Mingo County teacher Katie Endicott put it as follows: "We love our unions; we couldn't have accomplished what we did without them. But we did have to overstep them along the way at certain times."

An indispensable ingredient in the victories of West Virginia and Arizona was the existence of a "militant minority" of workplace activists—that is, individuals with a class struggle orientation, significant organizing experience, and a willingness to act independently of (and, if necessary, against) the top union officialdom. Though few in number, young socialists inspired by the Bernie Sanders campaign played an outsized role. Given the illegality of strikes in these states and the unions' long-standing reliance on lobbying the Democrats, it's not surprising that radicals were the only political current willing and able to consistently fight for a sustained work stoppage.

Much of this behind-the-scenes story has gone unpublished until now, since strike leaders in the heat of battle were understandably reluctant to give Republican red-baiters further ammunition to denounce the movement. But analyzing the impact of workplace militants is essential if we want to extract political lessons from the strikes and make sense of why they developed differently in each state. The absence of a layer of militant teacher organizers in Oklahoma, for instance, goes a long way toward explaining the relative weakness of its walkout. Without experienced grassroots activists to point the way forward, the Sooner State's explosive upsurge fell short of its potential.

Comparing West Virginia, Arizona, and Oklahoma reveals the continued relevance of an old insight: the revitalization of working-class struggle, and democratization of the labor movement, depends to a significant extent on the active participation of radical unionists and socialists. Labor needs the Left—and the Left needs labor. This isn't because leftists are any smarter than anybody else, but because class struggle perspectives correspond best to the actual structural challenges and political opportunities facing working people.

By leaning on the accumulated experience of labor's past and an inspiring vision of a better future, socialists throughout US history have usually played a central role in rank-and-file insurgencies. Indeed, the modern trade union movement arose in large part from the tireless organizing of Socialists, Communists, and Trotskyists prior to and during the Great Depression.

But the deep links forged between socialists and the labor movement were subsequently severed by McCarthyism, trade union bureaucratization, and the Left's turn away from workplace organizing. Fortunately, it appears that this imposed divorce—which has been equally damaging for both US trade unionism and socialism—may be coming to an end. In 2012, socialist activists, in alliance with other class struggle unionists, played a key leadership role in Chicago's powerful education strike. On an even-grander scale, the red state rebellions have demonstrated that reuniting political radicalism and organized labor is both necessary and possible.

Sanders and Socialism in West Virginia

To understand how and when West Virginia's strike erupted, it's not enough to look only at worsening labor conditions. Since at least 2014, intense anger toward pay stagnation and premium increases for the Public Employees Insurance Agency (PEIA) had been the norm, without leading to any mass resistance. In the words of one demoralized teacher on the West Virginia Public Employees United Facebook page, "We have had several 'strike worthy' endeavors over the last few years and we've done nothing but take it."

Emily Comer, a native West Virginian and teacher in South Charleston who had been organizing around a variety of social justice causes beginning with Occupy in 2011, argues that it was the impact of a newly emerged layer of young leftist organizers that made this time different: "Of course, a lot of factors led to this strike. Our economic crisis is not new. But I think the biggest difference is that since 2016 we've been developing a network of radicals in West Virginia. You know, we're still pretty disorganized—but we had just enough cohesion and strength to step into the political vacuum after the latest attacks on PEIA."

The roots of West Virginia's militant minority are easy to trace. Outside of southern counties where labor traditions run deepest, each of the core organizers I spoke with pointed to Bernie Sanders's insurgent primary run as *the* critical turning point.

Sanders's confrontational politics and radical vision captured the imaginations of well over 100,000 West Virginian voters. At a sold-out mass rally on April 26, 2016, in Huntington, he announced, "We are going to create an economy that works for all of us, not just the people on top," exhorting West Virginia to "join the political revolution."

Nicole McCormick explains what this looked like in Mercer County: "I've been politically aware and involved with the union for probably at least the past seven or eight years. But really it was when Bernie started campaigning that I became heavily entrenched in the ideology that 'everyone deserves health care, everyone deserves a decent life.' That's when I really got hard-core about all this. Bernie put forward class politics in a way that was really approachable to a lot of people I work with. They didn't look at him as something scary: he was just saying we deserved a better life. He also made the word *socialism* stop being so heavily stigmatized."

On the night of his primary victory, after trouncing Clinton by winning every single county in the state, Sanders described West Virginia as "a working-class state" where "many of the people there are hurting." They know, he said, "like most Americans, that it is too late for establishment politics and establishment economics. They want real change." Aided by the machinations of the Democratic Party establishment, Clinton ended up getting the national nomination. But Sanders's primary run demonstrated that class struggle electoral campaigns could be a tremendous lever for building up the confidence and self-organization of working people.

Matt McCormick described how this played out in his personal experience. A few years earlier, bad working conditions while working at Walmart had led him to become "defiant, class conscious, and outspoken against [his] managers." Soon after quitting, he began exploring radical ideas. But until the Sanders campaign, McCormick felt politically isolated: "Before Bernie, you could only vote for Republicans or Democrats that act that like Republicans. When Bernie came along, now there was a glimmer of hope, because he was saying what we believed all along. Basically, my wife Nicole and I were democratic socialists before it was cool to call yourself that. We just didn't have an outlet for our politics. Bernie provided that outlet and gave a sense of legitimacy to our viewpoints."

In addition to spreading and legitimizing class politics, the Sanders campaign in West Virginia, as across the country, helped coalesce a new organized socialist movement in the form of a reborn Democratic Socialists of America (DSA).

One of DSA's most important young members in the state was Emily Comer. In her view: "The role of the Bernie campaign of 2016 on organizing in West Virginia really cannot be overstated. We didn't have a DSA chapter until Bernie. After his run, a few DSA chapters started to pop up around the state because Bernie's campaign had gotten folks really excited for class politics. And it got people, especially young people, plugged in who before had been feeling hopeless and who would not have made their way into organizing before."

Of all the people Comer met inside DSA, by far the most important was fellow Charleston educator Jay O'Neal. Though he's too modest to take credit, other West Virginian activists agree that O'Neal was largely responsible for coalescing the circle of radical teachers that first initiated the collective push toward a strike.

O'Neal's personal trajectory illustrates that many of West Virginia's key strike leaders were motivated more by political conviction than family tradition. Raised in a conservative evangelical household in Texas, he became disillusioned with Republicanism when President Bush invaded Iraq in 2003. After moving to San Francisco in 2011 to teach middle school, O'Neal joined the union, eventually becoming a building rep—"Honestly, I wasn't very good," he insists—and participating in a 2014 strike authorization vote.

The following year, he moved to West Virginia and promptly dove into the labor movement, soon becoming a building rep at his school and the union treasurer for Kanawha County. "I knew by that time that unions were important," he recalls. "And when I saw how bad our pay was, I was like, 'I *really* need to be involved.'" Initially confused by the existence of competing teachers' unions, he ended up joining the West Virginia Education Association (WVEA) over the American Federation of Teachers-West Virginia (AFT-WV), since the latter had already endorsed Clinton instead of Sanders.

"Bernie was huge for me—that label *democratic socialist*, it definitely stopped being scary," O'Neal explains. "And it felt like there was a real popular shift in West Virginia, Bernie was super popular here. But the Democratic Party establishment iced him out, leading to Trump's victory. After the election, like a bunch of other people, I said to myself, 'Man, I've got to do *something*.' So when I saw that there was now a DSA chapter here, I decided to check it out."

In the hope of coming up with a strategy to turn things around for public employees in West Virginia, he began discussions with Nicole and Matt McCormick, whom he had met at the 2016 convention of the National Education Association (NEA). O'Neal also reached out to leaders of the 1990 West Virginia strike, and he began reading everything he could about the lessons of the 2012 Chicago educator walkout, notably Micah Uetricht's *Strike for America* and Labor Notes' *How to Jump-Start Your Union*. But it was not immediately clear to him how to translate those experiences to "right to work" West Virginia.

Looking to find some answers, O'Neal set up a small DSA committee on labor and education in the summer of 2017, which Comer and a few of his progressive teacher friends joined shortly thereafter. Its most consequential decision was to organize a study group on Jane McAlevey's *No Shortcuts*, a manual and manifesto for working-class strategy. "We decided to read *No Shortcuts* because we saw the state of organized labor in West Virginia: we keep losing, our unions are dying, and PEIA keeps getting more expensive every year," Comer recalls. "We were in agreement that if something didn't change, we were done for, basically. We also agreed that new life could be breathed into our unions—and that as rank-and-file members, we were strategically placed to lead that push."

The main political upshot of the book for Comer was its "clear analysis of the difference between real organizing and advocacy." West Virginia's unions, she realized, were stuck doing the latter, which "didn't build real power." Reading *No Shortcuts,* in her view, "was a starting point for giving us confidence to begin organizing and to say: '*We* are the union. We're dues-paying members, we're not going to wait around for anybody else to change things for us.'" O'Neal agreed with this assessment, adding that "*No Shortcuts* was also really powerful because reading it made us realize: 'Hey, socialists are *usually* at the front of a lot of big labor battles and strikes!'"

Armed with these insights, Comer and O'Neal were well prepared to respond when the latest changes to PEIA were announced in October 2017. Before exploring these initial organizing efforts, it's worth noting—contrary to red-baiting stereotypes about nefarious radical infiltrators—that they had no intention of secretly manipulating public employees to impose a "socialist agenda." Rather, the ethos that guided the two was Marx's affirmation in *The Communist Manifesto* that socialists "have no interests separate and apart from those of the working class as a whole." Socialists in West Virginia and across the country were not aiming to divert the working-class struggle; they were just trying to help it win. In fact, Comer and O'Neal both bent over backward to make sure that the movement "stayed organic," as they liked to say.

The truth is that even if DSAers *had* wanted to try to control the education movement, their nascent grouping was too weak to do so. As a recently formed "big tent" organization with little established infrastructure and few experienced activists, West Virginia's DSA was hardly a well-oiled machine. If anything, this was a significant drawback: at no point did Comer, O'Neal, or the McCormicks have the benefit of a cohesive political structure to which they could turn for organizational resources, tactical advice, or collective initiatives. Insofar as they received any outside counsel, it was from individuals like former AFT-WV organizer Ryan Frankenberry and, after January, Ellen David Friedman of *Labor Notes*.

Comer sums up the situation as it stood in the fall of 2017: "We had a small group of active socialist teachers with a strategic analysis doing organizing on the ground across West Virginia—that was crucial. But it was *so* important that we always worked alongside other people who were not socialists. There's no way we could have done this on our own."

First Steps

The first few months of the fight for a PEIA fix were an uphill battle. It seemed like 2017–18 could very well end up like school years prior, during which employees vented their anger about rising costs without taking any substantive action. With Republicans in power locally and nationally, many educators and union leaders felt that nothing could be won before the November 2018 midterm elections.

Charleston's cluster of DSA teachers took a different approach. Comer explains: "Last October, when the latest changes to our health care came down, we immediately knew that with this Republican legislature, it was going to take something really big to win. Our goal was to do whatever it took to beat back these attacks and fix PEIA. Realistically, we saw that this could very well could require a strike—or at least a credible strike threat. We didn't know what would happen; we didn't know that it would *have* to come to that. But we knew that it *could*. So we were definitely talking strike from October onwards. But our goal wasn't a strike per se, our goal was to win. Either way, we knew that we needed to begin with a bunch of escalating steps to build up power."

O'Neal decided in late September to create a Facebook group with him and Comer as co-moderators. As is the case with most serious organizers, O'Neal was just trying to replicate what he saw work well elsewhere: "Honestly, I got the idea to form the group from my experience participating in DSA's New Members Facebook group. It's funny, because that DSA page ended up getting pretty out of control, but at least it made me see that social media could actually be used to build an on-the-ground movement."

For Comer and O'Neal, the main purpose of West Virginia Public Employees United was to create a forum through which workers from different unions could join together to begin collectively organizing. In Comer's words: "It's strange: union leaderships here in West Virginia often spend more time trying to compete with each other for members than they do fighting the boss. So we needed to get around the fragmentation—we weren't going to get anywhere with three separate orgs with three separate strategies."

Seeking to build the broadest possible working-class unity, Comer and O'Neal also chose to heed Ryan Frankenberry's suggestion to make it a group of and for all public employees, rather than just teachers. Without this early decision, it's hard to imagine the chain of events leading to the state's eventual granting of a 5 percent raise to every public employee. The fact that Comer and O'Neal made it a *statewide* Facebook group was no less consequential. By eventually uniting educators in all fifty-five counties, the movement constituted a significant advance over the 1990 strike, as well as over the localized WVEA walkouts that had sprung up in 2007.

Nevertheless, in the first month of its existence, the group didn't "catch." To O'Neal and Comer's dismay, few people were joining or commenting. It was only after they took clipboards and sign-up sheets to PEIA informational hearings in November, and began bird-dogging politicians in December, that membership began to steadily grow. By the end of the year, 1,260 had joined the group. In early January, O'Neal and Comer chose, adroitly, to make the United page "secret"—you could only join if another public employee first invited you—which gave the group a certain mystique and cohesiveness.

The United page's lightly moderated, freewheeling discussion style led to more than a few unfounded rumors, a source of considerable consternation for its moderators. But generally the group page worked well, particularly since it could tap into West Virginian educators' relatively rich reserve of trade union experience and knowledge. By late January, West Virginia Public Employees United had grown to over 20,000 members.

Without social media, there's no chance that the red state revolt would have developed as it did. Facebook made it possible to communicate easily with large groups of people and to widely disseminate calls to action without, as in the past, having to undertake the arduous task of building up a well-resourced, formal organizational infrastructure. Rather than idealizing (or dismissing) the impact of this new technology on social movements, it's better to view it as a double-edged sword.

On the one hand, social media gave rank-and-file activists the ability to widely—and rapidly—disseminate calls to action across the state. It also changed the relationship of forces between them and their union leaderships. Without relying on official union channels, individual teachers from far-flung counties were able to share with one another their concerns, information, and ideas.

But on the other hand, the ease of mobilization and communication provided by Facebook has real downsides. In the Internet age, mass protests can scale up very quickly— sometimes *too* quickly for powerful organizations to develop in the process. Without the political relationships and infrastructure forged through in-person organizing, protest movements that rely on social media can be structurally fragile and ill-equipped to confront either harsh ruling-class opposition or serious internal debates.

Social media mobilization also poses important challenges to internal democracy within movements. Unlike in the trade unions, leaders of the red state educator Facebook groups were completely self selecting. Though educators could be polled online about next steps, and though they could vote with their feet by ignoring or leaving the groups, the ranks had no ability to select—or remove—their moderators. In West Virginia this never became a big issue, since the United page did not try to serve as a decision-making body. Oklahoma's and Arizona's Facebook leaders, in contrast, *did* make important political decisions during the walkouts, which raises all sorts of difficult questions about democratic process and accountability.

This divergence points to a broader point: social media can be wielded by organizers in very different ways. Oklahoma's grassroots leaders, for example, focused most of their energy on Facebook, underestimating the urgency of building up to a strike through escalating workplace actions and collective organization. In contrast, Comer and O'Neal were school-site organizers who intentionally focused on getting educators to participate in protests, workplace actions, and union meetings.

"A lot of people across the country seem to have the impression that we just created a Facebook page, then 'Boom!' everyone went out on strike," O'Neal explains. "Actually, we used the Facebook group to share information about months of concrete buildup actions and meetings going on in real life. These activities generated momentum, which in turn fed more interest and participation in the Facebook group. The two built on each other."

Even in West Virginia, however, events surged forward so quickly that those militants across the state who sparked the strike lacked sufficient time to cohere themselves as a distinct statewide tendency. Partly, this was because so much of their on-the-ground organizational activity took place directly within the unions; O'Neal and the McCormicks, in particular, were important local union leaders. But the relative organizational weakness of the rank and file (and those on the Left in particular) proved to be a consequential limitation, if not a fatal one. This, however, would only become evident later on.

As O'Neal explained above, the United page served as the main platform to promote a series of grassroots-initiated actions to raise awareness about the changes to PEIA and build up confidence that these could be defeated. Throughout November 2017, the moderators encouraged educators to attend PEIA hearings and make their voices heard. Next, O'Neal and Comer asked educators to write to their representatives. Nasty or dismissive Republican replies were soon plastered across the page.

In December, they stepped up their campaign by organizing, and frequently live-streaming, in-person confrontations with leading Republican politicians. Next, Comer and O'Neal crashed the governor's January 10 State of the State address by holding up a banner inside the capitol entrance that read: "Public Employee Healthcare, NOT Corporate Welfare! Fund PEIA now!"

The United moderators—most of whom were union building reps—did not limit themselves to promoting actions at the capitol. Their energy was equally dedicated to building up awareness and power at school sites and within the unions across the state. For his part, O'Neal barraged his coworkers with updates and calls to action at the end of each faculty senate meeting.

One particularly effective means to build workplace solidarity and momentum was to wear the same color shirt on a given day. On January 26, West Virginia Public Employees United organized the first statewide "Red for Ed" day: educators at hundreds of schools wore red and posted group photos on the page. The unions continued this tactic in the coming weeks, and it would later spread to Arizona and across the nation. A week later, on February 2, O'Neal and Comer took the initiative to organize the state's first walk-ins, an idea first floated by local union leaders. It was significant that these actions began in Kanawha County, the heart of political power in West Virginia and the state's largest county. Kanawha had been a major weak link during 1990; the prospects of a truly statewide strike would be dim if it were to remain aloof again this time.

Together with such activities, the United moderators engaged in constant political discussion and agitation. Initially, their main goal was just to get out information about the latest attacks against public employees. Soon they combined this with specific calls to resist, as in the following November 28 post by O'Neal: "For the last few years, I've gone to the PEIA hearings. People get angry, and then we go home . . . I refuse to let that happen this year without more of a fight. Let's work together to brainstorm some things we could be doing to hold our governor's and legislators' feet to the fire."

One of O'Neal and Comer's particular contributions was to bring the question of progressive taxation to the fore. In person and online, they hammered home the point that taxing the rich was the only viable way to fix PEIA. As O'Neal posted on December 17: "These tax cuts largely flow to out-of-state corporations. It's time to ask: Who does our state's leadership value more? Out-of-state corporations OR West Virginia's public employees?" By the time of the work stoppage, the idea that PEIA should be fixed by increasing the gas severance tax prevailed among public employees. During the nine school days of the strike, chants of "Tax our gas!" periodically erupted inside the capitol.

Another major emphasis of the United moderators was the need for rank and filers to participate in, and transform, their unions. Even in West Virginia, with its history of labor activism and its relatively strong union membership density in public education (70 percent), many workers were initially dismissive. Threats to stop paying union dues were common, as were arguments that it was a waste of time trying to work within these bodies. In response, the McCormicks, O'Neal, and Comer insisted over and over that unions were only as strong as their activated memberships.

A January 6 debate on the United page is illustrative. After one teacher denounced the union and called upon teachers to drop their dues, O'Neal responded: "WE ARE THE UNION. I know for a fact that when they went on strike in 1990 it wasn't because leadership wanted to—they were pushed that direction by their members. If we want to see real change in our unions, WE'VE got to make it happen."

It is difficult to overemphasize the importance of the fact that West Virginia's radicals were all active members (and frequently local leaders) of their unions. It meant that, for all the often sharp differences within the movement, there were always open lines of communication and coordination from the bottom to the top, and vice versa. Even well before they agreed to strike, unions were playing an important role by disseminating information about the proposed changes to PEIA and encouraging members to make their voices heard. And, particularly as the movement heated up, the structures of the unions served increasingly as a framework for grass-roots organizers to collaborate with statewide leaders on shared activities like walk-ins, rallies, and eventually the strike vote.

Above all, the main political contribution by West Virginia's militant minority was to drive forward the case for a work stoppage. The dominant image of West Virginia's walkout—as a purely spontaneous explosion—seriously underestimates how much hard work it took to overcome the fears of educators and the hesitations of their union leaderships. "It's true that we have a long tradition of unionism in West Virginia," notes Charleston teacher Olivia Morris. "But this was basically dormant until right before the strike."

The first mention of the "s word" came on October 6, when O'Neal posted news about the push toward a strike in Fresno, California. "We are settling for FAR TOO LITTLE here," he concluded. A skeptic replied that "WV teachers aren't allowed to strike," to which O'Neal responded: "True, but they did anyway in 1990 and it made a big difference." Over the coming months, this basic argument was repeated thousands of times in a myriad of iterations.

Advocates for the strike were unquestionably in the minority until February; new teachers and service personnel were particularly fearful. Matt McCormick recalls the dynamic at his school: "For weeks, there were these constant get-togethers in hallways and in mailrooms, where we'd discuss what the hell was going on. Lots of folks were initially scared, but I kept on repeating that it was worth the risk. People started asking each other: 'Would you go out if I go out?' There were some who initially said no, but they changed their minds—eventually."

By starting threads about the lessons of the 1990 strike, O'Neal sought from early on to help public employees consider the feasibility of a work stoppage. As he put it on January 6, "I think if we could educate more teachers about what the [1990] strike actually did for teachers here, we might get a lot of people on board." One of the key insights generated by these discussions was the centrality of involving support staff. "Striking again may not be such a bad idea," remarked a service employee who had been obliged to cross the picket lines in 1990. "But everyone must stand together and [in my opinion], this includes nonprofessional personnel also."

As things started to heat up in January, two members of the United group, in particular, drove forward the case for a strike: Matt McCormick and Mingo County's Justin Endicott. In fact, they basically refused to talk about anything else.

After another moderator on January 10 asked members how they felt about the governor's State of the State address, McCormick responded, "Public employees need to strike." Three days later, he elaborated on the point: "This won't stop unless we are willing to walk off the job together . . . We have to be willing to disrupt the state's ability to function." Endicott chimed in: "I agree 100 percent and if we don't it will only get worse . . . What will it take is the question I have been asking." When a fellow teacher responded that the real solution was to vote in favorable candidates in the coming elections, McCormick pushed back: "I don't think we'll solve this at the ballot box." Endicott put it similarly: "Until we draw the line we will face this every session from now until forever."

From January 16 onward, both Endicott and McCormick began calling upon the union leaderships to start taking concrete organizational steps toward a strike. Endicott put it like this: "Our unions aren't doing what they are supposed to be. Sending me a summary of bills and telling me to email my legislators is not what I pay them for. They need to walk in that building and start telling these legislators that they will pull us if it doesn't stop immediately." McCormick made a similar case: "[Union] leadership needs to indicate they are willing to take that next step. We need them to talk to county presidents and organize a ballot to determine interest in a sick out or strike."

By mid January, the United page and school sites across West Virginia were buzzing with talk about the feasibility of some form of job action. Until this time, the unions had done nothing to promote or facilitate this discussion—in fact, top WVEA officials had called O'Neal into their headquarters in October to request that he "work within the union" rather than the United page, which they feared was the embryo of a new union. Then, in early January, they called upon Matt McCormick to stop talking prematurely about a strike.

Under growing pressure from below, top union officials began to shift gears. On January 15, at a small WVEA rally to commemorate Martin Luther King Jr. Day, union president Dale Lee acknowledged, "I've heard a lot of people talk about 'It's time for a walkout or time for a strike.'" He argued for taking things slow: "If we were to get back to that, there's a lot of groundwork that needs to be laid beforehand." Comer recalls her and O'Neal's elation that the "s word" had been mentioned: "That night we were like, 'We got Dale Lee to mention the word strike!'"

Aiming to provide information to their members about PEIA and the legality of a strike, union leaders and staffers fanned out across the state. As AFT-WV lobbyist Bob Brown stated on January 29, an additional purpose of these trips was "to figure out what's going on" among the mobilized ranks.[1]

Allen Stump, WVEA's full-time organizer for southern West Virginia, explains the union's message: "When we started hearing rumors about a strike, our agenda didn't change. I'd say, 'In all reality, you may lose your job and there might not be anything we could do about it.' But at the end of the day, what I also told everybody was that 'whatever you all want to do, we will help you organize, and we'll support you, we'll have your back.'"

Many teachers were frustrated that their union leaderships did not take a more proactive stance. Nevertheless, the openness these leaders expressed toward supporting educators' desire for militant action constituted a major departure from the usual negative approach of US labor leaders toward strikes—especially illegal ones. Even ardent rank-and-file organizers commended their top union leaders' willingness to go along with, and provide considerable resources to, the upsurge. Since this was also the labor officialdom's approach in Oklahoma and Arizona, it makes sense to pause and examine the roots of this important, and rather exceptional, development.

---

1 Cited in Ryan Quinn, "Mingo, Logan School Employees Planning 1-Day Walkout; Others May Join," *Charleston Gazette-Mail*, January 29, 2018, wvgazettemail.com.

Some of the key factors were conjunctural. For one, the fact that Republicans were in power created considerably more room for maneuver, since unions could support a strike without having to break their ties to the Democratic Party. As the movements gained traction, union officials realized that these could be potentially important springboards to elect Democrats in the November 2018 elections.

No less important was the fact that these labor officials were operating in "right to work" states—conditions later imposed upon the entire US public sector by the *Janus* decision. The prerogative of workers to stop paying dues at any time—though weakening the trade union movement as a whole—creates a qualitatively different power relationship between union ranks and officials. If labor leaders hadn't heeded the desires of their mobilized members in these three states, the latter could have decided to just walk away. Indeed, threats among rank and filers to drop dues were prevalent throughout the red state rebellions.

It is also significant that in "right to work" industries without collective bargaining, workers can easily switch from one union to another. In West Virginia, for instance, fears of being outflanked by rival unions frequently spurred officials to talk and act more militantly than they might have otherwise. Union competition, while paralyzing in periods of demobilization, proved to have some significant benefits.

Finally, these states' prohibition of mandatory "agency fees" undermines labor bureaucratization by considerably lowering the number of full-time functionaries that unions can afford to hire. The fact that local union presidents were working classroom teachers, not staff materially dependent on union dues, made them much more responsive to their coworkers and more willing to take the risk of an illegal job action. In many ways, they functioned more like a powerful shop steward than a typical union president.

This doesn't mean we should promote or support "right to work" laws. Smaller union memberships, lower financial resources, and weaker organizational infrastructures are serious impediments to generating, and particularly to *sustaining*, working-class power. But contrary to widespread fears that *Janus* marked the death-knell of organized labor, it's worth keeping in mind that the "agency fee" is a relatively recent US institutional anomaly dating back only to World War II, when the state sought to prop up union officials who feared that their wartime no-strike pledge would lead to a mass outflow of dues payers.

In West Virginia, Oklahoma, and Arizona, the relative weakness of those institutional forces that normally channel or stifle labor discontent created more space for rank-and-file activists to promote workplace action. Ironically, it is precisely these sorts of political conditions that the Right is actively seeking to generalize across the United States through anti-union attacks like *Janus*.

Criticizing Republican Supreme Court justices for scoffing "at the issue of labor peace," AFT President Randi Weingarten explained in the wake of the *Janus* ruling that "if you look at the places in this country that have robust collective bargaining, you've seen very few strikes and work stoppages in the public sector, because they solved those problems at the bargaining table. Now, those problems will be solved in different ways."[2]

The Southern Counties Rise

By the end of January 2018, there was a lot of talk in West Virginia about walking out. But it was still just *talk*. Union leaders were noncommittal, and many educators remained fearful. As late as January 29, one could still find frequent posts like the following on the United page: "This group will accomplish nothing. All I read is whining and complaining. If people are upset, they have the right to be, but a call for a strike every three or four posts is going to accomplish nothing, especially since we don't have the right, too."

It's fitting that the initiative to move from words to deeds came from southern West Virginia, where a century-long tradition of labor militancy still looms large. The deep continuity of labor traditions—projected onto West Virginia as a whole in the national media coverage of the strike—*does* still exist in counties like Mingo, Wyoming, and Logan. To quote Katie Endicott: "Mingo—we're the home of Matewan, the Mine Wars, the Battle of Blair Mountain. This is our history, this is in our blood. Everybody here knows somebody who's been on strike."

Few people today are aware that the coal miner battles that culminated in the 1921 Battle of Blair Mountain—the

---

2   Cited in Hamilton Nolan, "Randi Weingarten Has 'Hope in the Darkness.' And Also Some Fear," *Splinter News*, July 2, 2018, splinternews. com.

country's largest insurrection since the Civil War—were largely led by socialists. After subsequent governmental repression wiped out West Virginia's socialist movement, it was primarily through militant trade unionism that the radical spirit of the Mine Wars lived on over the next century. Thus, in Mingo, unlike Charleston, the firebrand teachers who spurred the recent education strike weren't socialists. As is often the case in areas with a strong labor legacy, the militant minority encompassed not only ideological radicals, but also rank-and-file organizers committed to (and capable of) leading class struggle on the job— including, crucially, against the hesitations of the top union leadership when necessary. Though all genuine socialists support class struggle unionism, not all class struggle unionists support socialism.

Numerous educators stepped up to make the strike possible. But in the southern counties, as in the rest of the state, it's not hard to pinpoint the inner core of dedicated organizers that played a vastly disproportionate leadership role. Three Mingo educators stood out in particular. One was Brandon Wolford, a sixth-year special education teacher in Williamson and president of the Mingo County WVEA.

The Wolford family's long history of coal mining and labor militancy played a central role in Brandon's upbringing: "This goes *way* back for me; it was instilled in me since birth. I was raised with an understanding that you stick with your coworkers no matter what—and that you *never* cross a picket line." Wolford proudly recounts that his grandfather was involved in the 1920 Battle of Matewan and that he eventually became local president of the coal miners' union in Columbus, Ohio, before getting killed in a 1947 slate fall.

Brandon's father, also a coal miner, had participated in the fifteen-month strike of 1984–85, a bitter and violent struggle marked by physical clashes, gunfire, jack throwing, slit tires, and truck barricade picket lines. These experiences had a profound impact: "My mom had collected a ton of low-quality VHS tapes about the strike, and I used to watch them for hours as a kid. It made me so proud that my dad had participated in those battles. You could say that it sparked a special interest—ever since I was little, I knew that I wanted one day to be in a struggle like that."

During the strike's buildup and development, Wolford's main organizer allies were Katie Endicott and her husband, Justin. Both were from proud union families—his in coal mining, hers in education. "My mom was on strike in 1990—I was just four years old, and I was out there on the picket line with her," Katie explains.

The Endicotts were also leaders at school and in the community. Though they were union members and participated in periodic activities in defense of education and public employees, their organizing experience and activities before the strike came largely through the church: "It was nothing new for us to mobilize people during the strike, because we've already done that, just in a different field. So even though we weren't very active in the union until recently, people here know us—and we already knew how to organize quickly and efficiently."

Despite the region's militant traditions, it took a long time before most workers in southern West Virginia were willing to fight back against the changes to PEIA. Active participation in the unions had been low for many years—and it remained so up through early 2018. Though some people mistakenly believe that the southern counties unilaterally sparked the strike, Katie Endicott is the first to note the importance of the preceding organizing efforts initiated by O'Neal and Comer: "We can't really overstate the importance of the Facebook page. It was the catalyst—it allowed us to get networked and get the pulse of all fifty-five counties very quickly." It was not until the third week of January that teachers in the southern counties began organizing in earnest.

A small group of Mingo educators, including the Endicotts and Wolford, had traveled up to Charleston to participate in WVEA's disappointingly small MLK day assembly on January 15. Sensing an urgent need to ramp up the struggle, Justin and Katie informally met that night with a few of their coworkers to discuss possible ways forward. "I told my husband, 'We need a union meeting—and it needs to be open to *everyone*,' " Katie recalls. "So he talked to Brandon Wolford, and within a couple of hours we had a meeting scheduled."

On January 23, over 250 Mingo County educators squeezed into the Carewood Center in Delbarton. The room was crackling with tension. Union staffers—Allen Stump (WVEA) and Brandon Tinney (AFT-WV)—began the meeting by informing the audience that statewide union leaders, though neither advocating nor discouraging an eventual strike, were against any immediate job actions.

Challenging his union superiors, Wolford, the Mingo County WVEA president, spoke forcefully in favor of a walkout. Never one to stay quiet, Katie Endicott took the floor to insist that the meeting set a specific date for the action: "We cannot leave this room until we decide on a date. Whether we realize it or not, the eyes of the state are on Mingo County. We just need a spark."

In the face of this outcry, Stump, like his AFT-WV counterpart, decided to cede to the assembled educators: "Who I am to argue with an entire county of workers? At least 90 percent wanted to walk out. One lady stood up and said to us, 'Listen you all can either get behind us or get out of the way, because if you don't, we'll run you over.'"

Mingo's assembly closed with a decision to set up school-site strike votes for a one-day walkout on February 2. Aiming to spread the job action, Wolford reached out to local presidents in neighboring counties, asking them to join in. Over the next three days, similar mass meetings were held across the south. Support for organizing a strike vote was virtually unanimous in Wyoming County, where the movement surged forward under the guidance of WVEA copresidents Tina Adams and Lisa Collins.

Four counties—Mingo, Wyoming, Logan, and McDowell—ended up walking out on February 2 and rallying at the capitol. Virtually overnight, West Virginia was set politically ablaze. "After that first walkout, everything immediately blew up," recalls Ashlea Bassham. In the words of another teacher, Carrena Rouse, "The tipping point came from the south." As Endicott had anticipated, their action sparked the flammable material gathered over the preceding months by O'Neal, Comer, and the other United moderators.

Endicott sums up this political dialectic: "We knew that unity was the keystone. So without the Facebook page I don't think you'd have ended up with '55 Strong.' However, without the Facebook page you'd still have ended up with February 2, because we organized that action on our own, outside that broader statewide dynamic. And February 2 was *such* a turning point—we fired them up."

The Strike

After February 2, the die was cast. Walk-ins and other school-site buildup actions expanded exponentially in all counties. Organizers called for another round of one-day walkouts in mid February, with seven counties participating. By this time, the upsurge had grown so large that it superseded the organizational capacity of West Virginia's militant minority.

In ever-increasing numbers, rank and filers beseeched their unions to call a statewide strike vote. After a few days of continued discussion, the leaders of the AFT-WV, WVEA, and West Virginia School Service Personnel Association (WVSSPA) responded positively. Leaning on their significant organizational infrastructure and a newly invigorated membership, the unions jointly coordinated strike authorization votes in every school during mid-February. Organized labor's tremendous power was beginning to be tapped.

Despite the state's attempts to head off a work stoppage by making significant concessions—among them freezing PEIA costs and repealing bills that introduced charters, undermined seniority, and eliminated automatic union dues deductions—the vote results showed overwhelming statewide support for a strike. Roughly 80 percent of educators statewide voted yes, and the yes votes were nearly unanimous in schools with a strong union presence. At the end of a massive and rainy February 17 union-led rally in front of the capitol, WVEA and AFT-WV presidents Dale Lee and Christine Campbell announced that all school employees would be walking out the following Thursday and Friday, February 22 and 23.

By taking responsibility for the authorization votes and the strike, West Virginia's union officials had finally placed themselves at the head of the upsurge. The unions' significant financial, organizational, and political resources were immediately deployed to make the action a success. Militant organizers in Mingo and around the United page saw this as a very positive development, since they had never aspired to substitute themselves for their unions. At the same time, the schoolsite votes had made it clear that the strike's legitimacy and authority should rest ultimately on the workers' democratic decisions. This set an important precedent—one that would later come into play when strikers defied the labor officialdom's premature decision to call off the strike.

Regarding the strikes' health care demands, however, West Virginia's militant minority proved too weak to win. Everybody was in favor of a permanent "fix" to PEIA, but what exactly this entailed—and how it would be paid for—was left unspecified by union leaders. The United moderators, with the help of State Senator Richard Ojeda, had succeeded in widely disseminating the proposal to raise West Virginia's natural gas severance tax. Yet this had not been formally adopted as a demand for the strike. Jay O'Neal explains: "From October onwards, we had been arguing that the only solution was progressive taxation. But the union stuck with its stance that 'it's not our job to figure out where to come up with money.' We knew that this was a problematic line because if the solution was left up to our politicians, they'd try to screw us."

In O'Neal's view, these ongoing ambiguities concerning how to fix PEIA were directly related to the organizational limitations of West Virginia's militant rank-and-filers: "Honestly, my main regret of the strike is that we didn't have a strong statewide structure of like-minded educators, through which we could have formulated and won things like a clear set of demands, particularly around taxing the rich and corporations. We moderators were always on the phone with each other, and we talked about demands—but from January onwards we just got so busy and overwhelmed, we weren't able to really push this through."

The rank and file may not have been strong enough to push through a progressive PEIA fix, but they *did* save the day by ignoring their union leaders' premature commands to return to work on the evening of Tuesday, February 27.

When I spoke with AFT-WV President Christine Campbell after the strike, she was open about acknowledging this: "We should have given ourselves processing time, to know where the members were at. And, honestly, when we went out to the crowd on the steps to make that announcement, we just didn't know. So if I could take back one day in my last six years of being union president, it would be that Tuesday. But I'm grateful to the membership for deciding to stay out."

Together with thousands of their coworkers, West Virginia's militant minority immediately began agitating Tuesday night to keep the strike going. After the union announcement from the steps, Matt McCormick posted the following definition on the United page: "Just FYI: 'A wildcat strike action, often referred to as a wildcat strike, is a strike action undertaken by unionized workers without union leadership's authorization, support, or approval.'" Over the next twenty-four hours, the Facebook group was inundated with comments, questions, and updates. Tanya Asleson recalled that "everybody was on the United page—that's how we could tell that most people weren't ready to go back."

In-person gatherings on Wednesday were also critical. The scene at the capitol that morning was absolute chaos— nobody knew what was going on and rumors were flying that the governor had resigned. Katie Endicott relates how Mingo County educators intervened: "Everybody was coming up to us asking, 'What's Mingo doing?' We explained that we weren't going back, we didn't care what Dale or Christine had agreed to. We didn't know if our superintendents would call off school, but it didn't matter— we weren't cooling off."

At 1:00 p.m., Charleston educators and union representatives packed into a church down the block to deliberate. The room was far past capacity, with hundreds of people crammed into the pews and aisles. Kanawha County's AFT-WV president, Fred Albert, opened the meeting with a prayer along the following lines: "Dear God in heaven, give all of us during this trying time the guidance, clearheadedness, and strength to trust in our union leadership in guiding us through this storm."

If Albert believed that this prayer was going to shield the union leadership from criticism, he had badly miscalculated. County union presidents tried their best to make a case for the deal, but they received nothing but heckling from the crowd, prompting the beleaguered AFT-WV president to storm out in anger. From her perch next to the podium, Emily Comer soon after texted the following update to a fellow organizer: "This guy from WVEA who looks like a basketball coach is telling us we need to go back in to protect us from an injunction. People are SHOUTING."

In an interview the following day, Jay O'Neal told me that the meeting "got really heated, quick. I think teachers let out their frustration. Honestly, I was worried that the meeting might spiral out of control. But then a teacher from the floor spoke up and said: 'We want to vote, we want to decide when to go back in.' This really expressed where people are at." To their credit, Kanawha's local union leaders eventually apologized and ceded to their ranks' desire to democratically decide on whether to stay out.

In Kanawha, as in counties across West Virginia, educators that afternoon and evening voted overwhelmingly to continue the strike. Unconvinced that superintendents would respect their decision, many educators also began planning hard picket lines, beginning at four the next morning, to physically prevent any attempts to open the schools with scabs. Emily Comer, who by this time was functioning as de facto building rep, recalls that "frantically organizing those pickets was definitely the most terrifying moment of the strike—I think it was actually the most scared shitless I've ever been in my life." In counties across the state, other organizers undertook similar preparations.

Because West Virginia's radical organizers were swimming with the political tide during this critical juncture, it's difficult to measure their immediate impact on the wildcat. Most educators were so fired up, mobilized, and organized by this point that defiance of the union leadership would probably have occurred even without concerted efforts by the militants.

Developments in the debate over the PEIA health care program point to the challenges West Virginia's radicals faced in helping guide the tempest. On Tuesday night and Wednesday morning, the main reason given by rank and filers for rejecting the deal was that the governor had promised only a task force, rather than a lasting fix, for PEIA. Yet by Thursday, most educators had changed their tune: the strike, they now argued, had to continue until the agreement between the union leaders and Governor Jim Justice was signed into law.

There were various reasons for this evolution. Most importantly, after Republican Senate leader Mitch Carmichael rejected the deal on Wednesday, many educators concluded that it was necessary to win the deal first and a PEIA fix later. But there were also other factors at play, including the United moderators' continued abstention from a struggle around demands. Comer explained that "staying out on strike for a PEIA fix would have meant a simultaneous fight versus the union leadership *and* the state, and honestly we didn't feel we were strong enough for that."

O'Neal makes a similar point: "Because the strike didn't have clearer demands from the beginning—particularly on progressive taxation to fix PEIA—it made it hard not to accept what we were given in the deal. In hindsight, maybe we could have tried to push for an independent task force (instead of one handpicked by the legislature), but particularly given how chaotic things were on Wednesday, I'm not sure we were sufficiently organized to pull that off."

That this deferral on a PEIA fix was the strike's major limitation shows how high expectations had been raised in the course of struggle. By this time, educators had already forced politicians to back down from the proposed health insurance changes that had initially fueled the movement, as well as the bills introducing charters, attacking seniority, and instituting anti-union "payroll protection." When the Republican Senate caved on Tuesday, March 6, by giving an across-the-board 5 percent raise to all public employees, the educators' ecstatic response was well warranted.

Taking a step back, it's evident that the influence of West Virginia's militant minority evolved over time. Their role was greatest in the first four months of the struggle, during which they took the lead on promoting mass actions, building statewide public employee unity, and overcoming the hesitations of top union officials. Once the movement exploded after February 2, and the union officialdom stepped into leadership, the relative importance of organized radicals receded somewhat, in part because the movement as a whole became so militant.

Like most successful labor struggles, West Virginia's strike arose from the self-activity of countless workers combined with the conscious interventions of experienced organizers. One individual who understood this better than most was WVEA President Dale Lee. During the spontaneous victory celebration on the morning of Tuesday, March 6—as throngs of educators inside the capitol embraced and cried from joy—Lee unexpectedly walked up to Emily Comer, shook her hand, and said in a low voice: "*You* did this." Whether this was meant as praise or a reprimand was left unclear. Either way, Lee was right that the rank and file—with the help of its most tireless and fiery activists—had made history.

Oklahoma's Missing Militants

Few things are more dangerous to the ruling class than the inspiring precedent of a successful labor action. After West Virginia, political expectations were raised virtually overnight; educators all across the country began to realize that it was possible not only to fight, but to win. Mickey Miller notes how the mood among Oklahoman educators was transformed: "Oklahoma teachers have felt hopeless and powerless for years. So when I first heard about West Virginia, I didn't think it would spill over for us. But teachers here started closely watching the strike. They began saying, 'Wait a second, they did it there, they were able to get all counties to go out. Why can't we do that here?'"

At most times, the conscious intervention of radicals or experienced organizers is required to transmit lessons from organized labor's past into today's movements. But because West Virginia's successful strike had taken place so recently and was so widely publicized over social media, some of its key political takeaways diffused widely in Oklahoma, even in the absence of a militant minority.

West Virginia was a powerful inspiration, but it had also made winning look a little too easy to outsiders. Many educators seemed to get the impression that all you needed for a successful strike was a lot of anger and a Facebook group. Lost in the breezy national media reports were the months of organizing—and the political strategies that informed these activities—that made West Virginia's success possible. As we will see, the strategies and tactics through which West Virginia educators and their unions came out on top remained hazy for the rank-and-file activists that initiated Oklahoma's work stoppage.

The main limitation of Oklahoma's strike—and its main point of divergence from West Virginia and Arizona—did not concern the amount of pay won from the state. Hoping to avert an imminent work stoppage that had been called for April 2, the legislature on March 29 passed a revenue bill that promised to give teachers a raise of roughly $6,000, or about

15 percent. This was a major achievement, particularly in a state that had not increased taxes a single time since 1990. The adopted revenue bill, however, included only minimal funding increases for schools, and a modest raise for support staff and state employees. Unlike in West Virginia and Arizona, the work stoppage itself was unable to wrest any added concessions from the government.

Moreover, Oklahoma's walkout made few gains in terms of building up the collective organization or self-confidence of working people. These organizational weaknesses—culminating in the implosion of the work stoppage in mid April—can to a great extent be traced back to the limitations of Oklahoma educators' contending leaderships, both on the union and grassroots levels. By the time the walkout ended, teachers were hardly more organized than they had been at the beginning of the movement; moreover, a feeling of demoralization was pervasive.

If West Virginia provides a positive example of the importance of a militant minority, Oklahoma's experience shows what can happen in the absence of such a layer of experienced radical organizers. Though a new socialist movement arose in Oklahoma following the Sanders campaign, none of its members were educators—in marked contrast with those in West Virginia and Arizona. As we'll see below, the ensuing political vacuum among Oklahoma's rank and file was subsequently filled by individuals with no organizing experience and no connections to the unions.

The First Steps

All regions of this country have their own rich traditions of radicalism, though much of this history has been buried. It's a little-known fact that a century ago, Oklahoma had the strongest Socialist Party in the country. It was not until the state's deployment of vicious repression during World War I that it was finally able to destroy Oklahoma's mass socialist movement. In 1925, seeking a complete eradication of the leftist legacy, political leaders replaced Oklahoma's red state flag because it was too associated with working-class radicalism. Only the state motto, "Labor conquers all," remained as an artifact of Oklahoma's radical roots.

The present-day rebirth of a socialist movement in Oklahoma can be traced to February 28, 2016. On that Sunday afternoon, Bernie Sanders electrified a rally of over 6,000 in Oklahoma City. "We have a message that speaks to working-class people," Sanders declared. "Whether you're conservative, whether you are progressive, you understand we're in a rigged economy, where ordinary Americans work longer hours for low wages and almost all new income and wealth is going to the top 1 percent."[3]

As in West Virginia, Sanders dominated the 2016 primary. Xavier Doolittle, a member of DSA in Tulsa, recalls the campaign's catalyzing effect on the state: "Bernie showed how radical Oklahoma was under the surface. Those rallies

---

3   Juliana Keeping, "Bernie Sanders Rocks Crowd of Supporters in Oklahoma City," *The Oklahoman*, February 28, 2016.

when he came really inspired and electrified people. He won the Democratic primary by a huge margin—and he gave an outlet to the deep dissatisfaction that existed with the status quo. People who had been isolated now felt confident and mobilized."

Since 2016, Oklahoma's socialist organizations have grown steadily. Indeed, by early 2018 the number of organized socialists in the Sooner State was similar to that in West Virginia. But there was one big difference: none of these Oklahoman DSAers had jobs in the schools. For this reason, they were unable to transmit class politics or organizing know-how into Oklahoma's education movement, either during the lead-up to the walkout or once it had begun, and they were limited to providing outside support.

After West Virginia's strike erupted, two separate rank-and-file initiatives sought to give expression to Oklahoma educators' growing desire for action. The first was Oklahoma Teachers United (OTU), a Facebook page driven by Tulsa teacher Larry Cagle. Founded in 2017, OTU had attempted to build support for some localized sickouts by Tulsa teachers in early 2018. But the group had only a few visitors until West Virginia's strike caught the country's attention by going wildcat on February 28.

The second, and much more influential, Facebook page was Oklahoma Teacher Walkout—The Time Is Now! (TTN), created on February 28 by Stillwater teacher Alberto Morejon. Within hours, the membership of TTN had shot up to 18,000—and in a matter of weeks, it had become

Oklahoma's most influential rank-and-file hub, with over 70,000 members.

Focused on the same public education demands and the same action proposals, TTN and OTU were differentiated more by style than by politics. Politically, both of their founders were somewhat eclectic: neither had any previous organizing experience, neither were members of the union, and neither raised demands around progressive taxation. Though he radicalized over the course of the movement, initially Cagle proudly announced to all that he was a "fiscal conservative." For his part, Morejon was a registered Republican for whom party labels mattered less than a demonstrated commitment to supporting teachers and improving Oklahoma's public schools.

Both pages also consciously sought to spread and implement what they saw as the key lessons of West Virginia. As Morejon explained to me, "We learned a lot from West Virginia; it set a precedent." Above all, each page stressed that a walkout was necessary and that it would only come about through the independent initiative of Oklahoma teachers.

However, the two Facebook pages differed substantially in tone. OTU, like Cagle himself, was brash. For example, he declared to the press on March 2: "If we strike, I double dare you to fire us. We'll just go to Texas; they're looking for new teachers."[4] This bravado endeared OTU to some of the most

---

4   Burt Mummolo, "Oklahoma Teachers Planning a Statewide Strike," *KTUL*, March 2, 2018, ktul.com.

fired-up teachers, but it also ruffled a lot of feathers in a state known for its politeness, and in a workforce that prides itself on professionalism. Smaller questions also played a role in the eventual relegation of OTU to second fiddle—educators, for example, periodically complained of the moderators' use of profanity and spelling errors. As one teacher exclaimed on March 7, "Profanity is not necessary to make a point!"

In contrast, TTN's widespread popularity reflected Morejon's more positive, professional, and matter-of-fact style. Oklahoma teachers came to trust Morejon as an honest individual and as a leader. In contrast to West Virginia's United page, only Morejon could make posts to his group—others could only respond to polls or make comments under his posts. A tightly moderated Facebook page had the major benefit of being much easier to follow than West Virginia's page, which was often overwhelmed by a flurry of posts on various topics. Nevertheless, the fact that TTN was unabashedly Morejon's project was not conducive to collective strategizing or organizing.

On the whole, Cagle and Morejon's political similarities outweighed their differences. Both seized the moment and pushed for bold action. Yet their lack of organizing experience had important consequences for the movement. So too did their disconnect from the Oklahoma Education Association (OEA)—the state's the main union, representing roughly 40 percent of school employees.[5]

---

5   Oklahoma also has an AFT chapter, which organizes teachers in Oklahoma City. But, like in Arizona, the AFT was far smaller and played no independent political role in the movement or walkout.

The union's controversial decision to end April's walkout after nine days has cast a long shadow. But it's necessary to underline that OEA shared the same political and tactical approach of its counterparts in West Virginia and Arizona. For many years now, it has been focused on fighting for better pay and more school funding, primarily through lobbying and electoral campaigns. Though these efforts have been generally unsuccessful, they did succeed in fending off some of the worst attacks and in keeping the crisis of education firmly in the public eye.

If anything, the depth of the state's education woes made OEA somewhat more proactive about supporting a walkout than were its labor counterparts in West Virginia and Arizona. By early 2018, Oklahoma's union leaders had already been discussing the possibility of organizing a walkout for close to a year. That such plans for a potential job action were not made public, however, reflected both the prevailing hesitation of the OEA leadership to pivot toward mass action, as well as its ongoing difficulties in communication with its members and the public. The Republican dominance of state governance—a big difference from 1990, the year of the last teachers' strike in Oklahoma—considerably lowered the officialdom's expectations in what a job action might realistically be able to achieve. For these reasons, OEA did not initiate the type of systematic organizing drive usually necessary to prepare for a successful strike.

The first real initiative for a job action came from the grass roots. In the summer of 2017, a group of teachers in the small town of Bartlesville started pushing for a statewide walkout around pay and funding. After the February 12, 2018, legislative failure of the most recent bipartisan education funding plan, these teachers' idea for action was floated by Bartlesville's supportive young superintendent, Chuck McCauley. He sent out a poll asking how many of his fellow superintendents and school boards across the state would support a teacher walkout.

With talk of a work stoppage beginning to percolate, OEA President Alicia Priest jumped in. On February 19, she announced to the press: "When we walk out, it is for our kids. And, we've got to do better. And, so, it may be time again soon." Four days later, OEA posted the following poll to its Facebook page: "The Oklahoma Legislature has repeatedly failed to adequately fund education or fund pay raises for teachers and education support professionals. Is it time for a work action?"

This post gives a good sense of OEA's stance on the eve of the red state revolt. Yet it wasn't widely publicized, nor was it a significant spur to the eventual walkout. Nevertheless, with a willing union, two viral Facebook groups, and the inspiring example of West Virginia, it seemed in the first week of March as if the stars were aligning for a powerful strike in Oklahoma.

The Date Debate

Events moved extremely quickly from this point, and talk of a walkout dominated the press and school sites from March 1 onward. Indeed, West Virginia's strike had not even ended before Oklahoma's movement was plunged into a fractious internal debate that would have a decisive impact on the course of its movement. In the span of a few chaotic days, pivotal decisions were taken that set into motion the walk-out's key organizational failures.

Conflict centered around the question of what date the work stoppage should begin. Morejon and Cagle wanted April 2; OEA initially wanted the first week of May. Though many Oklahoma educators, as well as numerous leftists across the country, celebrated the eventual victory of the rank and file's date, it turned out to be a Pyrrhic victory.

The proposal for April 2 had been generated in private discussions between Morejon and Bartlesville superintendent McCauley. Since McCauley didn't have the reach or inclination to organize a mass mobilization, agitating for the date had depended entirely on the grassroots Facebook leaders. On March 3, Morejon had blasted the April 2 date out to his group and received an overwhelmingly enthusiastic response. While it had initially floated even earlier dates for a strike starting in March, ultimately Cagle's OTU also fought for April 2.

Significantly, neither Morejon nor Cagle raised the perspective that the decision to stop work should be voted on at school by all employees—each moderator, instead, relied on Facebook comments and periodic online polls of their groups to gauge interest in a strike. Nor did OTU or TTN argue during these crucial first days that the walkout should be organized through, or in close collaboration with, OEA— of which neither Morejon nor Cagle were members.

Instead, their early focus was on having teachers reach out to superintendents and work with them directly. As Morejon announced on March 2: "The goal is to allow superintendents and school board members to discuss the possibility of a school shutdown/suspension until something is done . . . I will be organizing a day next week where everyone in this group will email their districts superintendent and school board members to ask them where they stand on this issue." On March 4, Cagle's OTU similarly posted that it was "in discussions with superintendents from across the state in hopes of unifying our efforts so there is [a] single voice representing teachers."

In the early-March rush of excitement, the problematic implications of this approach were appreciated by few teachers. But without school-site votes to decide on a work stoppage, it remained unclear who had the ultimate authority to start or stop the action. As the course of the walkout would later demonstrate, the absence of such votes resulted in a very different relationship of forces between employees and superintendents—and between rank-and-filers and top union officials.

Looking back at this issue months later, educator Stephanie Price made the following self-critique: "I honestly feel like we gave too much power to the districts to determine our plan for us—we were basically waiting for our superintendents to give us permission to walk out. We allowed ourselves to sit back and wait to until we were told, 'Yes, you're allowed to walk out.' We should have just said, 'We're doing this.'"

To be sure, organizing independently of—and if necessary, against—superintendents would have subjected educators to more legal risks than a district-sanctioned walkout. But one of the key lessons of West Virginia was precisely that if you have the numbers, it's possible to break anti-democratic labor laws and win.

Convincing Oklahoma educators—and pressuring the union—to take such a risk, however, would have required a concerted effort on the part of grassroots leaders. It would have also taken a considerable amount of time for organizers to test school employees' strike readiness—particularly support staff, for whom a walkout necessarily entailed greater financial and job-security risks. There were certainly many thousands of teachers on the two Facebook pages who were already eager to strike at the soonest possible date. But that was still only a fraction of the total workforce. Neither TTN or OTU seem to have perceived any urgent need to deepen the movement's organization at school sites or in more conservative towns before setting a date for a walkout. Unfortunately, experience would soon demonstrate that the types of personal-organizational relationships and difficult political conversations necessary for establishing real workplace power can't be forged solely through Facebook.

OEA shared some of these same strategic limitations—including a hesitancy to move beyond organizing a legal, superintendent-sanctioned walkout. But union leaders also perceived that building for a successful work stoppage required more on-the-ground efforts and more time than the four weeks projected by Morejon and Cagle. "That was just too soon for a successful job action," recalls Amanda Ewing, associate executive director of the OEA. "Alberto was new to politics and he had absolutely no conception of the amount of work, and amount of time, it takes to make something like this happen. Basically, we thought that it'd be impossible to get to the point of a real strike by April 2. Having a date in the first week of May would have given us the ability to have really laid the groundwork for support, and to have bolstered our members' courage to walk."

There were additional tactical reasons why the OEA considered a later date to be preferable. First, because federal funding is contingent upon completion of standardized tests, walking out after mid-April state testing would avoid a situation in which teachers could be pressured to call off the strike. Second, the legislative session ended in late May. Ewing explains: "We wanted to choose a date so that we could stay out until the end of the legislative session or the end of the school year if necessary. With our initial proposed date of early May, we knew might have to stay out for at least four weeks. The plan was to stay out, if necessary, until the end— but to do that, starting in April was just too long of an ask to make of educators. You'd have to potentially stay out for eight weeks to hold the politicians' feet to the fire."

On March 5, OEA President Alicia Priest and Executive Director David DuVall reached out to Cagle and Morejon to see if they would consider the possibility of working together around a later date. As a compromise, OEA changed its proposal to April 23.

Ewing notes the uneven success of the union's conciliatory efforts: "In the hopes of collaboration we reached out to both groups—at various points. Our president and director called Larry early on, when things started moving very quickly and we were trying to figure out the best date for the walkout and how to get people working together. But that conversation quickly devolved into Larry screaming, 'You work for me!' to us, even though he's not even a member of OEA. We came away with the impression that he wasn't someone we could work with—plus it was becoming clearer to us that though he was loud, he didn't really have the capacity to mobilize people."

For his part, Cagle saw OTU's intransigence as analogous to the militancy of West Virginia rank and filers. But whereas radicals in the Mountain State had openly identified with the union and called positively on its leadership to listen to the ranks, Cagle took a more strident approach. Looking back at the course of the movement, Cagle later acknowledged, "I now know that I must be a leader within the union to help create the change I desire."

OEA's conversation with Morejon was more cordial. As he recalls, "My whole thing was, I didn't want to cause any divisions. I spoke with the union and, to be honest, for a while there I was willing to do whatever the union wanted to about the date." On March 6, he posted a note vaguely indicating an openness to the April 23 compromise. But he didn't make a case to his followers in favor of moving to a later date—and, given the excitement already generated for April 2, at this point it would have taken a concerted push by Morejon to have convinced riled-up educators of the benefits of a slower approach. Instead, Morejon posted soon after: "This Group showed OEA that April 23rd was too late. They listened to us!"

Eventually, OEA realized that it had no choice but to cede to the pressure for April 2. "We knew we'd look ridiculous changing the date," explains Ewing. "But we decided: 'It's going to happen with or without us, so we need to help.'" In a widely publicized March 7 video message, Alicia Priest announced that the union was calling for statewide school closures "beginning April 2—we will be at the capitol until a solution is passed and signed by the governor . . . Our members are ready to act now, so we are accelerating our strategy."

The Strike

The wind was at the backs of Oklahoma educators, but three weeks was not a lot of time to build for a work stoppage. It didn't help that the forces pushing for the walkout were doing so largely in isolation from each other. Neither Cagle nor Morejon sought to merge their groups or coordinate their activities, and relations between OTU and OEA only continued to worsen over the course of March.

In comparison with OTU, there was somewhat more unity between Morejon and the union, at least at first. In a good faith OEA effort to build collaboration, Morejon had received an invitation, which he accepted, to speak at the joint press conference to announce the April 2 walkout. But beyond that, they did little to unify their efforts and messaging. When I later asked Morejon and OEA leaders about the reasons for this ongoing disunity, each pinned the blame on the other side, charging their rivals with an unwillingness to cede control and leadership over the movement. Perhaps both were partially right. The date debate had crystallized a mutual suspicion, rooted at least partially in an underlying divide between nonunionized workers and the OEA.

Above all, their lack of coordination reflected the slanted organizational relationship of forces. Despite its concession in the April 2 debates, the OEA did not feel compelled to coordinate walkout organizing, because neither OTU nor TTN was attempting to work proactively within the union (as in West Virginia), or to build an independent organizational base (like in Arizona). When I asked why they hadn't coordinated more, one union staffer (who asked to remain anonymous) argued, "Basically, the union saw that though the Facebook groups were popular, they weren't doing real organizational groundwork for the walkout."

In the lead-up to April 2, Oklahoma's two competing Facebook pages did their best to generate enthusiasm for the work stoppage. Largely through digital agitation, they helped spark a flurry of local actions to get the word out to parents and community members, and to coordinate with superintendents. Morejon's Facebook group continued its upward ascent in traffic. But little systematic in-person organizing was attempted at school sites or beyond.

To many rank-and-file teachers, it seemed like the growing tide of social media–induced mobilization would be sufficient to make the Republicans concede all along the line. Stephanie Price later reflected on this question: "At the time, it felt like we were moving forward, but looking back I feel like we were far less organized than the other states that struck, Arizona in particular. When I eventually found out that they had liaisons at every school, it made me wonder how effective we could have been had we built that kind of organization from the start in our strike process."

The first test of strength for the movement came on Wednesday, March 26, when the state legislature passed the funding bill HB 1010xx in a last-ditch effort to head off the imminent walkout. This was a significant win for teachers; had it not been for the credible strike threat, there's no way that the Republican legislature would have raised taxes or conceded such a large raise. But, like in West Virginia and Arizona, concessions by politicians on the eve of the walkout proved to be insufficient to head off the grassroots upsurge. Overwhelmingly, Oklahoma educators were adamant about sticking with their planned work stoppage in order to win better school funding.

After HB 1010xx, however, both the superintendents and OEA began to waver. Across the state, superintendents showered praise on the bill, and for the first time, they began framing April 2 as a one-day rally only. OEA's response to HB 1010xx was also somewhat equivocal. On Wednesday evening, the union thanked the legislature and declared that the "historic" bill was "major progress." But it added that there is "still work to do to get this legislature to invest more in our classrooms. That work will continue Monday when educators descend on the Capitol." With this politically adroit move, the union pivoted away from a focus on pay demands by foregrounding the fight for funding.

Initially, OEA's leadership, like many superintendents, appeared to be trying to avoid an ongoing strike by transforming April 2 into a one-off action, after which teachers would return to work. The unattained demands could then be fought for through less disruptive means. But it was also clear that union leaders didn't trust the legislature, and that they were worried about getting overtaken again by the rank and file. Indeed, Morejon's response to HB 1010xx was uncompromising. On Thursday, he insisted that the bill was "not enough to prevent the walkout" and posted the following call to arms: "We teachers control our destiny! We have come too far to accept this offer that does nothing but put a bandaid on a severe wound."

The union leadership quickly stiffened its spine. In a new video update on the eve of the walkout, Priest declared, "We will stand with our members as long as our members want." By Monday, April 2, OEA appeared to have decided to stay out for at least several days to pressure the legislature to make further concessions.

Whatever OEA's limitations, it is hard to imagine the movement reaching the point it did without their active support. It put serious organizational and financial resources toward the walkout. And it frequently pushed hard for big turnouts at the capitol, as did Morejon.

Perhaps the most incredible aspect of the walkout was its massive size, given Oklahoma's weak labor organizations and traditions—a limitation compounded by the absence of any systematic workplace organizational buildup during March. One certainly cannot attribute the divergence of Oklahoma's movement from West Virginia and Arizona to lower levels of educator militancy or mobilization.

Tens of thousands of teachers, plus a sizable number of public employees, demonstrated in the cold on Monday, April 2—a far larger crowd than at any of West Virginia's rallies. That Monday evening, some teachers privately worried that turnout in the coming days might decline. Amazingly, the opposite occurred: Tuesday's and Wednesday's numbers were each greater than the day before. And Monday, April 9, was the largest action yet, with an estimated 50,000 at the capitol. At the walkout's height, about half a million students— roughly 70 percent of the state total—were out of school.

These massive turnouts took place despite OEA's rather-unclear stance on funding demands and next steps. Though OEA leaders were personally in favor of progressive taxation, the union's actual policy proposals remained scatter-shot. Morejon recalls that "it seemed like every day OEA was changing its demands—it was really confusing and teachers were getting upset."

Amanda Ewing provided her take on OEA's approach: "A lot of what we were doing was focused on logistics: how to set up parking, how to get people inside the capitol, setting up Porta Potties, all that. But my main regret is that we could have communicated better. This was true in general, but particularly for nonmembers: we basically didn't have an infrastructure to communicate with non–OEA members."

Underlying these difficulties, however, was OEA's reluctance to fight for a clear platform on progressive taxation—or to encourage educators to stay out until their funding demands were met. Morejon's post on Thursday, April 5, went viral: "Does OEA want us to give up so they can say . . . 'Well we at OEA tried'? Are the Legislators waiting us out, or is OEA waiting us out? When is the last time OEA clearly announced what would end this walkout without being extremely vague?"

Throughout the entirety of the work stoppage, Morejon remained by far the most influential force encouraging teachers to stay out until their demands were met. In contrast, in a video message on Tuesday, April 10, Alicia Priest began setting the stage for a pivot to the November elections: "If we've learned anything during this walkout, it's that we can't afford to continue to elect candidates that are dismissive of the needs of our students."

Like their counterparts in West Virginia and Arizona, OEA leaders tended to hold, and publicly project, low expectations about what could be won from a Republican legislature. It often felt as if union officials were treating these work stoppages as massive ongoing lobby days, rather than as strikes meant to *force* the other side to concede by creating and deepening a social crisis.

Nick Singer, who was asked by OEA to work as the capitol action's DJ, notes his frustration: "I kept on telling the OEA folks I knew, 'It's necessary to change the game, we've got to think outside the box.' Some were sympathetic, but they weren't used to bold, or deep, organizing—and they were getting a lot of bad advice and pressure from the staffers the NEA had flown in, who kept on insisting that it wasn't possible to win anything more and that it was necessary to wrap things up. So instead of redefining what was possible, instead of changing the relationship of forces through a compelling message of taxing the rich and corporations and an escalation of tactics (for example, calling on public sector workers to join in), OEA leaders just seemed to let the strike die with a whimper."

The political strategies of OEA and NEA officials were not the only factor weakening the walkout. Morejon was a celebrity among educators at the capitol, yet neither he nor OTU had any significant ground game or organizational presence. Once people were physically assembled together en masse, the limitations of an infrastructure based purely on Facebook became more glaring.

The lack of participation by service personnel was another significant weakness. Price noted that "this really hurt the walkout, because think about how many paras and support staff there are in Oklahoma—that's a huge loss of numbers. And in terms of solidarity, not having everyone participate in the action set up a sort of an invisible barrier between us."

Above all, the movement's ongoing reliance on a strategic bloc with district administrators did not prepare teachers for what would happen after April 2, when their erstwhile allies began pulling back. Though initially most superintendents and school boards remained publicly supportive of the walkout, behind the scenes they were, to quote Singer, "really seriously undermining the action—honestly, they were the biggest cowards." By the end of week one, with state testing looming, district leaders—including presumed allies like Bartlesville's Chuck McCauley—began pressuring employees to return to work. Ewing notes, "By having chosen to start on April 2, we created a timing risk that people hadn't fully contemplated."

Resistance to these pressures was possible—indeed, teachers in districts like Moore fought hard to stay out. But without strong workplace organizations, or the political precedent and authority generated by a rank-and-file strike vote, this task proved to be exceedingly difficult.

By Thursday, April 12, most urban districts remained out, and the public remained more supportive than ever, with approval ratings of over 70 percent. But in the absence of clear leadership from OEA or an organized effort from below, crowd numbers at the capitol were beginning to decline. So was momentum. The work stoppage had gone on nine days, the same length as in West Virginia, and Republican lawmakers still showed no signs of budging.

It was in this context that OEA officials, at a Thursday-evening press conference, abruptly called off the walkout. Nominally, they made the decision on the basis of a poll OEA sent to its members the preceding Monday. But that vaguely worded survey hadn't specifically asked educators whether they wanted to end the walkout—and moreover, many union members, not to mention the majority of educators, had not received it.

Teachers across Oklahoma were outraged at OEA leaders. Hundreds dropped their dues, and incensed teachers immediately inundated social media with denunciations of OEA for "betraying" and "selling [them] out." One of the more measured responses on April 12 came from teacher Gabrielle Price, who posted: "I'm upset, I'm tired, I'm frustrated. I was used, I was thrown under the bus, and I was misrepresented." She expressed the sentiments of many in a tear-filled video post that went viral:

I appreciate OEA. They have provided shuttles, bathrooms, they have provided awesome things for us, which is great. However . . . I didn't get a poll [to go back]. I was never asked on whether or not I thought the walkout should continue. There aren't a ton of union members, but I am a member and I was never asked about ending the walkout . . . This was a teacher-led walkout. This was not any organization's walkout. This was not OEA's decision for us to go fight. This was our decision.

It's hard to know for certain whether it would still have been possible, as of April 12, to turn around the walkout's momentum. Organizationally, the movement was already relatively weak. Yet the large school districts remained shut, and thousands of teachers, including the ever-vocal Morejon, remained convinced that it was still possible for the walkout to win.

Others, like Nick Singer, felt that the union should have stuck it out past April 12, even if there was no guarantee more concessions would be won. In his opinion, deepening and consolidating the movement's gains regarding mass organization and political consciousness didn't hinge on winning more state funding: "OEA leaders misplayed their hand. Who knows whether we could have forced the Republicans to back down, but the union definitely could have stayed out at least another week by highlighting a clear progressive funding proposal—like raising the capitol gains tax—and mobilizing hard for teachers to fight for it. We could have made the Republican leadership die on the hill publicly defending an inequitable tax structure to the death. And then, even if we didn't win, at least teachers would have been mad at the Republicans instead of the union. If we had gone out fighting, OEA and the movement would have come out a lot stronger."

On Friday, April 13, thousands of teachers scrambled to keep the walkout going. As Morejon put it, "The grassroots effort that started the walkout had to continue it." In an important move toward in-person organizing—one that would have been more effective weeks earlier—he called a mass meeting of teachers that Friday to determine how to move forward. Thousands crowded into the capitol to collectively discuss next steps. For a brief moment, it seemed like Oklahoma teachers might go wildcat, like those in West Virginia. But the hastily assembled ranks didn't have the organizational capacity to overcome the decision of OEA's leaders. By the following Monday, the walkout had petered out, though many individual teachers called in sick, and hundreds of schools began sending small delegations to the capitol.

Angered by the failure of the walkout to fulfill its potential, many educators concluded, defensibly, that the struggle could have advanced further had it been led differently. As Gabrielle Price put it: "In a movement this large, leadership is necessary. Unfortunately, the management that rose up was not the leadership we had hoped for."

The main problem, as I've tried to show, wasn't the approach of OEA officials, per se. West Virginia, and later Arizona, showed that the internal dynamics of the strikes hinged, above all, on the role of the rank and file. Oklahoma's insurgent teachers, however, found themselves insufficiently organized to overcome the hesitancy of their union leaders. Had the ranks been stronger, OEA would likely have been pushed to continue to support the upsurge.

Nor would it be fair to pin the blame on Morejon and Cagle. As individuals lacking the benefit of any previous organizing experience, they did the best they could to push things forward, and they stuck their necks out, often at great personal cost. Morejon's efforts, in particular, played a critical role in raising educators' desire to fight and in forcing Republican lawmakers to grant teachers a historic pay raise.

What was missing in Oklahoma was a team of like-minded grassroots militants, armed with activist know-how, class struggle politics, and an orientation toward working within the unions to push them forward. Indeed, this was one of the main lessons learned by DSA members in Tulsa and Oklahoma City. "The experience of our walkout really put into urgent focus for me that socialists can't effectively raise class consciousness from the outside," explains DSA organizer Xavier Doolittle. In the hopes of being better placed to help guide the Sooner State's next round of labor militancy, he decided in the wake of the walkout to become a teacher: "I saw that if you're not on the shop floor, if you're not an educator in public education, it's hard to be a credible messenger to workers in struggle. During the walkout, we tried our best to help provide solidarity from the outside, but it's just not the same as organizing alongside your coworkers."

Doolittle's confidence in the potential power of radical workplace organizers was not misplaced. Arizona's strike, the most remarkable work stoppage of the entire wave, would soon make this clear.

Arizona's Militant Minority

Few states in the United States have been more inhospitable to labor and the Left than Arizona. As Arizona Educators United leader Rebecca Garelli notes, "Arizona is ground zero for Koch brothers money, ground zero for charters, ground zero for vouchers, ground zero for privatization. We're in the thick of it, and we're up against a massive wall. I knew it existed, but it's greater than I ever imagined."

Precisely for this reason, the unexpected success of Arizona's 2018 mass strike serves as a perfect test case for demonstrating the importance of a radical militant minority. Arizona educators faced an even harsher political context, with even weaker unions, than did those in Oklahoma. Thus, for the purposes of a comparative analysis, Arizona's best counterpoint is Oklahoma rather than West Virginia, since the latter's relatively strong labor movement and traditions are a confounding factor that buoyed its work stoppage.

Like the action in Oklahoma, Arizona's strike arose directly in the wake of West Virginia. But the paths of the two movements quickly began to diverge. Since Arizona was an even tougher objective political context for mass labor militancy than Oklahoma, the greater success of its movement can best be explained by the subjective factor of political leadership. And given that union officials in both states shared a basically identical political approach, the most important differentiating factor was the orientation and experience of grassroots leaders. Through their efforts, Arizona's rank-and-file organization not only grew stronger than its equivalents in other states, but also superseded the influence of Arizona's official education union. "Arizona's walkout wasn't just random teachers stumbling in the dark," explains Noah Karvelis. "Teachers with experience and politics were helping guide this."

The Buildup

By virtually all possible metrics, the challenges to successful strike action were greatest in Arizona. Its right wing was considerably stronger, and its labor movement significantly weaker, than in Oklahoma—not to mention most other US states. Home of pioneering reactionary Barry Goldwater, Arizona has for many decades been at the vanguard of the conservative Right's offensive against working people. A whole host of regressive policies—ranging from tax cuts for the wealthy to school privatization to racist anti-immigrant crackdowns—have been tested and refined on the backs of working-class Arizonans.

The state's leading politicians are deeply embedded in, and indebted to, the Charles Koch Institute and the American Legislative Exchange Council, a hyper-conservative Koch-funded corporate legislation mill. Governor Doug Ducey has been part of the Koch network since 2011 and received $1.4 million from it in 2014 for his gubernatorial run. In 2017, more than a third of Republican legislators were wined and dined at ALEC's annual summit to promote "free market" model legislation.

Decades of one-sided class war have left their mark on Arizona's labor movement, which has long been one of the weakest in the country. Unlike Oklahoma and West Virginia, Arizona had never experienced a statewide teachers' strike. A "right to work" state since 1946, its union membership density is 5.2 percent, even lower than Oklahoma's 7.1 percent. The Arizona Education Association (AEA) represented only 25 percent of the workforce at the beginning of the 2017–18 school year, whereas in Oklahoma the rate was 40 percent, and in West Virginia it was 70 percent.

The particularities of Arizona's decimated public education system make it especially hard to organize. About 17 percent of Arizona students attended a charter school in 2018—more than three times the national average. In Arizona and elsewhere, charter employees remained disproportionately absent from the spring 2018 walkouts due to their lack of either job security or collective organization. The same was true for Arizona's large number of noncitizens working on J-1 visas to fill the state's teacher shortage.

Divisions over race and immigration status were also heaviest in Arizona. With a working class stratified by language and ethnicity, and a xenophobic Republican Party with significant roots among white workers, one could hardly choose a less hospitable area of the United States to build working-class unity. Until Red for Ed erupted, Arizona was more marked by individualism and xenophobia than collective action and solidarity.

In the face of these obstacles, it's highly unlikely that Arizona's movement would have scored so many victories without the tireless work, tactical savvy, and strategic clarity of Arizona Educators United. From March through May, each of the teachers who came to comprise the AEU leadership team threw aside much of their normal life in order to organize the movement. As Vanessa Arredondo-Aguirre notes, "It was crazy—those were some very long hours, it was nonstop. Every day, I'd get out of work and I'd be up 'til at least midnight organizing."

AEU was a collective effort, in which all of its core leaders—not to mention its thousands of rank-and-file local school-site activists—played an indispensable part. For the purposes of understanding the group's particular trajectory and impact, three activists played an especially outsized leadership role: Noah Karvelis, Dylan Wegela, and Rebecca Garelli. Even more effectively than Jay O'Neal and Emily Comer in West Virginia, this militant minority of young workplace organizers was able to lead mass struggle forward by leaning on their organizing experience and class struggle perspectives.

Like many living in Arizona, Karvelis, Wegela, and Garelli were raised in other states. Arizona, with its relatively buoyant economy, has for many years been a leading recipient of US working-class in-migration, particularly from the Midwest's stagnant Rust Belt. Indeed, in 2017 Maricopa County, Arizona, was the fastest growing county in the United States.

Notwithstanding this steady growth in blue state transplants, Arizona has remained a bastion of conservatism. In such a context, it's pretty extraordinary that someone like Karvelis could become the public face of a mass movement supported by millions. Faced with vicious red-baiting from the corporate media and Republican leaders, Karvelis was reluctant to publicly ascribe to ideological labels during the strike. But when I asked him how he wanted to be identified in this book, he replied, "Call me a democratic socialist, please."

Karvelis was raised in rural, working-class Illinois. His first inkling that something was wrong with the system came in the eighth grade. "Growing up where I did," he explains, "everyone was working class, most worked in factories. My family was single income and, after the 2008 recession, my dad all of a sudden lost his job, forcing him to look for work for many months. It was eye-opening: I realized we're all living at the will of these CEOs and investors."

During high school, Karvelis dug deep into political theory and history: "After my dad got fired, I got into *really* into reading about politics, to make sense of what happened—it was a pivotal moment for me to develop class consciousness." As for so many millennials, Bernie Sanders's 2016 presidential run was the catalyst that convinced Karvelis to get engaged: "That was a huge thing for me. Bernie's campaign showed me a new set of politics, that there was something beyond just being a Democrat—you *could* really fight for working class people and marginalized people. It was one of the first times that I'd seen anything happening in US politics that resonated with me, that reflected the things I believed in. It felt personal, it felt fresh, and it spoke to the problems of my family and my friends. So it was a really big moment for me—it was the first time I really volunteered on a campaign or got involved in politics."

Upon arriving in Phoenix to start teaching music, Karvelis immediately threw himself into in a wide range of local activist efforts and began writing publicly about education and politics. This political immersion, he notes, was indispensable for his later contribution to Red for Ed: "I've been reading and writing about all these issues for a while now, so that background definitely helped me get the movement off the ground."

Eager to seize the opening created by West Virginia, on the morning of March 1, 2018, Karvelis issued a soon-to-be viral call over social media for educators to wear red that coming Wednesday: "West Virginia is showing the entire nation what can happen when teachers stand in solidarity. Arizona's teachers are taking note and realizing that now is the time for us to start organizing our campuses and districts. Join us next Wednesday by wearing RED for ED and stand in solidarity with our demands for fair pay! AZ's teachers and schools deserve proper funding!"

Dylan Wegela received far less notoriety than Karvelis in the spring of 2018. But as the site liaison coordinator and the main strike proponent within AEU, his contribution to the movement was certainly no less important. Like Karvelis's, Wegela's politicization began early on. "Part of getting into politics was that I grew up in a very white part of Michigan and people sometimes treated me a bit different because my skin was tan," he notes. In high school, Wegela read some Marx and, though he was still skeptical, "the idea that there could be something different to capitalism resonated with me."

But it wasn't until college, with the Sanders campaign, that he actually got involved in organizing. Soon after diving deep into canvassing, he organized his first action—a keg party to raise funds for Sanders. Wegela recalls that the campaign was a game changer for him personally: "Bernie definitely made me call myself a democratic socialist; I had socialist ideals already, but honestly I hadn't even heard the label until the campaign. And it showed me that a large number of people actually wanted to fight to improve things. Those massive rallies convinced me that something had to change. So when I started teaching [in 2016 in Arizona], I got immediately involved here."

In the fall of 2016, Wegela decided to speak out at his school and in his district against the 1 percent raise received by teachers. Soon after, he was asked by veteran teachers to run for the executive board of his district union. By the spring of 2017, he was secretary of the Cartwright Education Association. "I learned a lot through this union work," Wegela emphasizes. "It made everything during Red for Ed way easier because I already had organizing experience—though not on that scale of course."

Rebecca Garelli took a different path toward becoming a militant leader. Like that of Mingo County's rank and filers, Garelli's radicalism has been focused squarely on union and workplace struggles. Though she had attended a few protests during college against the war in Iraq, her politicization took place primarily through participation in the radical-led Chicago Teachers Union (CTU): "That union militancy—for me it all comes from Chicago. I have a strong personality to begin with and even as a nontenured teacher I spoke my mind a lot. From my personal experience with issues at school, filing grievances and all that, it became clear to me *real* quick how powerful and necessary a union was. So I got involved: I'd go to all the union meetings, I'd wear my red shirt every Friday, I'd engage in all the activities they asked us to do."

Above all, it was Garelli's participation in the 2012 Chicago education strike that set the stage for the central leadership role she'd go on to play after moving to Arizona five years later. For her, the strike was a watershed moment: "That was an incredibly powerful experience for me. I didn't realize the full strength of our union until the organizing began for the strike. It was real democratic unionism. People who weren't political—it made them political. And it sparked such camaraderie and solidarity in our building. Then when we were actually on strike, marching in downtown Chicago—it was epic. We were under the high-rises and we'd see workers everywhere—all the buildings, on all the floors—supporting us, waving, holding signs. And the union every day told us, 'You have a job to do today.' We always had a task, it created this sense of unity—and it politicized a lot of people in the process."

Encouraged by the inspiration of West Virginia, on Friday, March 2, 2018, Garelli decided to start a Facebook page to mobilize and unite Arizona's educators. Within hours it had thousands of members: "The minute I created that page, it blew up. It was just supposed to be a discussion page, I consciously hadn't put any talk about striking in the description. But, immediately, people on it were like, 'YES, we're going on strike!'"

Until this point, events in Arizona paralleled those in Oklahoma very closely. And in both places, decisions made at this early juncture, and in the heat of the moment, determined much of the movement's subsequent trajectory. But, unlike her counterparts in the Sooner State, Garelli had enough union experience to realize the dangers of going too far, too fast: "The page was out of control. Lots of people on it wanted to strike—*now*. But I said, 'No way, there's no way we're ready yet for that!' I knew from Chicago that we had a lot of work to do before we were ready for something like a strike, particularly a statewide action. I tried to sell people on this perspective, but I saw what was happening. So that Sunday I posted that I was going to take the page down—we needed more time to prepare, to do this right. People were begging me and reaching out to me, 'Please don't shut it down, don't let the momentum die!' But I pulled the trigger."

After Garelli announced her intention to close down the page, Derek Harris—a young Tucson District band teacher and progressive union activist—set up Arizona Educators United to serve as its replacement. By Monday, March 5, nine teachers had come through a process of voluntary self-selection to serve as the AEU leadership team.

Spread out across the state, all were strangers up until this point. Most were young, with at most a few years of activism under their belts. Contrary to conspiracy theories hatched by Arizona's leading Republicans, AEU was hardly a socialist plot. Far from being ideologically monolithic, most were progressive Democrats, and there was even one Republican. Moreover, none of the teacher radicals were members of any socialist organization, unlike in West Virginia.

That Monday evening's conference call—the first of many over the next two months—divvied up coordinating tasks. For some in the team, including Vanessa Arredondo-Aguirre, Catherine Barrett, and Brittani Karbginsky, this was their first foray into activism. In contrast, Kelley Wendland Fisher was a longtime teacher and an experienced progressive union leader. Fisher notes that "as an 'elder statesmen' so to speak, in the first few days and weeks I did a lot of listening and not a lot of speaking in AEU—I let these new young leaders find their places first." Though her approach was mostly hands off, her role as a "conduit" between the two organizations was significant: "During the first weeks, tensions were high on both sides at times, and being able to talk openly to people in both groups really helped create a bond."

While Fisher and others focused on tasks like community outreach and building a digital platform, Garelli was mandated to strategize actions, Karvelis was made media spokesperson, and Wegela was charged with heading the (soon-to-be critical) site liaison network.

In contrast with Oklahoma's precipitous calls for a walk-out, AEU leaders decided to begin by systematically building a base at schools and in the community. To this end, the meeting decided to promote Karvelis's call to wear red across the state that coming Wednesday. Even more importantly, it adopted Garelli's proposal to build a structure of workplace representatives. She noted that the idea came directly from her CTU experience: "You have to set up a real organization on the ground so that when you hit the 'go' button, you hit with power."

By that evening, Wegela had blasted out a call for site liaison volunteers. Over the coming weeks, it would take count-less hours to input contact information, respond to volunteers, and provide them with ongoing guidance on how to organize their sites. Garelli helped get the system off the ground in early March, as did Arredondo-Aguirre. But the site liaison network—which by late April was comprised of roughly 2,000 educators—was above all Wegela's responsibility.

As he explains, "When Rebecca made that proposal for a site liaison network, I immediately knew that coordinating it was an important role and that I wanted to be that line of communication. Because of my experience as union secretary, I had picked up how to coordinate with members and help them get things done. And it turned out that the liaisons were the most important part of the movement. They organized their schools, got a sense of where people were at, and served as the channel of communication between the rank-and-file and our AEU leadership team. We couldn't have done any of this without them."

Anybody interested in how a militant minority of workplace radicals can build workplace power and political momentum should closely study AEU's two-month organizing blitz, most of which was done in conjunction with the union. With the help of AEU's new liaisons, thousands of teachers participated in the first Red for Ed day on March 7.

Karvelis recalls the profound transformation that this action had at his workplace: "When we organized that first Red for Ed day at my school, it was a real hush-hush whisper campaign to get it off the ground. People were still pretty scared to speak out and our district is notorious for being pretty complacent. But we ended up having 99 percent of educators decked out in red. That set the tone for the rest of the year—we've done it every Wednesday since, as did most other schools."

Based on her Chicago experience, Garelli envisioned and coordinated a series of escalating actions aimed at empowering educators and building support among community members. She also added some important tactics to the playbook. One of her personal innovations was to call on educators and allies to use erasable window markers to draw supportive messages on their cars, small businesses, and homes. By the time I arrived in Arizona, the state was awash in Red for Ed signs and decorated cars. "These might seem like modest asks," Garelli explains, "but they helped overcome the fear factor, and they helped people feel less isolated. You can't just do this overnight. If you don't have the confidence to do small actions, how are you ever going to be able to do a large job action?"

In late March, AEU called upon its members—which now numbered in the tens of thousands—to collectively formulate their demands through a democratic, deliberative process. Following extensive discussions online and in the school sites, these were then presented publicly at a mass rally of over 6,000 on March 28 at the state capitol. Next came a string of walk-ins that culminated on April 11, when over 110,000 educators, parents, and students participated across Arizona. By this time, the organizational strength and legitimacy of AEU had transformed it into a body more akin to a bona fide trade union than a loose rank-and-file network.

Though Arizona Educators United relied primarily on its site liaison network to coordinate and promote actions, it also utilized social media adeptly. Indeed, AEU leaders found a way to overcome the basic problem that had plagued both West Virginia and Oklahoma's pages: that if you open content up to anybody to post, a big group gets overwhelmed and the most important information tends to get lost; but if you restrict a page to moderator posts, then you lose the collective ownership and effervescence that made West Virginia's United page so attractive.

Initially, AEU had tried the Mountain State model, but, as Arredondo-Aguirre notes, "It was so big, there were way too many posts, and our information was getting missed." Their solution was to create a separate AEU "discussion hub" page where anybody could post, while making the main AEU page a vehicle for the leadership team's updates and asks—and for educators to post photos and ideas in the comments sections. Many AEU liaisons also created their own district-wide Facebook pages to facilitate local coordination.

AEU was also lucky to have a gifted public spokesperson. In interview after interview, Karvelis hammered on the same key points regarding Arizona's education crisis and the power of a collective fightback to solve it. Thanks to an uncanny ability to popularize a class struggle vision for defending educators and students, he immediately became a statewide celebrity. By late April, he could hardly walk two minutes without being besieged by strangers requesting he take a selfie with them.

Through two months of deep organizing, the movement had won over school employees from all political persuasions and in all corners of the state. Arizona educator Warren Faulkner's April 22 tweet illustrates the breadth of the popular radicalization:

I'm a registered Republican and a conservative. I've taught high school math for 27 years and the last thing I ever thought I'd do is a walkout, but I will walk out this

Thursday. Enough is enough . . . I love my job and I love the students I teach. I don't want to walk out, but I will for my students.

Red-Baiting and Socialism

Red for Ed's booming popularity and momentum would not go unchallenged by Arizona's Koch-funded right wing. For its efforts on behalf of educators and students, Arizona's militant minority was subjected to a relentless smear campaign. While there had also been ruling-class pushback in West Virginia and Oklahoma, it was nothing like this.

First, it was Governor Ducey who set the stage by refusing to meet with Red for Ed representatives, claiming on April 10 that they were "political operatives." Then, in the coming weeks, the powers that be threw every possible slander in their direction. Talk show hosts and politicians spuriously questioned AEU leaders' teaching credentials, their motivations for moving to Arizona, and their adherence to democratic norms when conducting the strike vote. *Fox 10 News* anchor Kari Lake even announced that Red for Ed was "nothing more than a push to legalize pot."

But above all, the tactic to which defenders of Arizona's status quo turned most was red-baiting. Pointing to Karvelis's involvement in the Sanders campaign and his authorship of online articles such as "From Marx to Trump: Labor's Role in Revolution," the twenty-three-year-old music teacher was their favorite target. On April 24, Arizona House Representative Maria Syms sounded the alarm in an op-ed accusing the entire education movement of being a socialist plot:

> If [Karvelis] gets [his goal], we will see contemporary radical politics at its treacherous worst, where harm to our children and their academic achievement are necessary collateral damage in the cause of leftist revolution. Arizonans should take a stand against such threats to our children and our democracy. We all deserve better. #TooRedForEd[6]

That same day, *Breitbart* published an in-depth account of Karvelis's purported attempts to brainwash his students with anti-capitalism and anti-racism.[7] The radical politics of some individual AEU leaders was now front-page news.

This demagogy fired up Arizona's crystallized reactionaries, confused the waverers, and took a toll on AEU leaders. "It's the hardest thing to stand up and know that you'll be smeared," recalls Karvelis. "But if you don't do it, who will?" Since he, like all of AEU's core, was sincerely committed to upholding Red for Ed's nonpartisan nature, Karvelis always tried to pivot the media's attention back to public education. In fact, if it hadn't been for these constant right-wing attacks, socialism would have been a complete nonissue in Arizona's movement.

---

6   Maria Syms, "#RedForEd Leaders Are Not as Nonpartisan as They Claim," *Arizona Republic*, April 24, 2018, azcentral.com.

7   Susan Berry, "Arizona Elementary Teacher Leading Strike: 'Teaching Is Political'," breitbart.com, April 24, 2018.

Red-baiting has long been effective as a right-wing tactic for discrediting and dividing labor struggles. As Karvelis noted in a 2017 article about working-class agency, the first "Red Scare," for instance, successfully extinguished "the fire at the heart of the labor movement . . . in its earliest stages."[8] Though Arizona's recent smear campaign did some real damage, it proved to be far less successful in undermining the struggle.

Unlike much of the rest of the United States since 2016, Arizona has yet to see democratic socialism become a mainstream idea. Nevertheless, most educators across the state pushed back in defense of Red for Ed and its rank-and-file representatives. It was not difficult to see that red-baiting was being weaponized against their demands for better pay and funding. Of course, a few teachers took the bait. Yet the vast majority insisted that their movement was a united effort of all supporters of public education, rather than a socialist plot.

Educators instantly took to social media with a wide range of rebuttals to the Republican smears. Many educators took offense at the implication that they were ignorant sheep manipulated by a wily conspirator. Others, likewise, stressed that this was a collective movement: "I love Noah Karvelis, but in kid language 'Noah's not the boss of me' . . . Noah didn't organize the standouts in Tucson or the other protests down here. We have tens of thousands of parents and community members and educators all organizing each other."

---

8   Noah Karvelis, "From Marx to Trump: Labor's Role in Revolution," *Medium*, February 23, 2017, medium.com.

Some posters noted that red-baiting was fundamentally a tool of the powers that be. In the words of one teacher, "Anything that benefits people that aren't rich is always marked as 'socialism.'" Others rejected the ideas of socialists but invoked their First Amendment rights. A few rank-and-file teachers even made cases for the positive importance of a radical presence in the struggle: "We are fighting a corrupt political environment and to purge ourselves of leftists seems authoritarian and stupid at the same time. You really think conservative Republicans are capable of leading the fight for change?"

One of the ironies of Arizona's smear campaign was that it prompted many educators to begin exploring radical ideas for the first time. As elsewhere in the United States, the content of the term *socialism* was contested widely in Arizona. Many equated it with public services like public education or the postal service. Others invoked *Wikipedia*'s useful definition: "Socialism is a range of economic and social systems characterised by social ownership and democratic control of the means of production, as well as the political theories and movements associated with them." A few argued that Jesus was a true socialist; Republican leaders like State House Representative Kelly Townsend, in their view, were Christians "in name only." A Phoenix teacher posted: "Kelly Townsend wagged her finger in my face and called me a communist at the Capitol and I took it as a badge of honor. Being the exact opposite of whatever she is is nothing to be ashamed of."

Arizona's red scare was not inconsequential. It peeled off some potential supporters, periodically put AEU leaders on the defensive, and created a climate conducive to the Republicans' efforts to ignore educators' demands. Yet on the whole, the Koch-backed Right failed to achieve its goal of turning educators and the public against AEU or its representatives. Teachers "voted with their feet" by sticking with Red for Ed.

Ultimately, the smear campaign's main long-term consequence will likely be that it helped generate a new audience for socialism in Arizona. A sign of just how far things had come in the span of two months was a May 4 *Phoenix New Times* piece titled "No, #RedForEd Isn't a Socialist Plot, but It Would Be Awesome If It Were." After discussing with Arizona's DSAers—who, like those in Oklahoma, were limited to building outside support for the strike—the author reached a conclusion common to a growing number of Americans: "If the leftist revolution that we've been warned about results in an energized labor movement and better funding for education, health care, roads, and other public institutions, that actually would be pretty great."

Relations with the Union

Though Arizona Educators United was both the spark and the primary leadership of Red for Ed, much of its success arose from close collaboration with the Arizona Education Association. As one rank-and-file teacher posted on April 21, "There is no way we could have come this far this fast without the AEA." Union officials committed significant resources to building the movement. And their collaboration with militant grassroots leaders was consistently closer in Arizona than any in Oklahoma or West Virginia.

Arizona's strike took a distinct trajectory despite the fact that AEA's political strategy was identical to its sister organizations in Oklahoma and West Virginia. Like most union officials I met during the red state revolt, AEA's top leaders were honest and progressive-minded individuals who were committed to defending public education, largely through lobbying and electing Democrats. Similarly, though they were willing to support the upsurge, their structural position made them hesitant to embark on an illegal work stoppage.

To understand the reasons for the exceptional alliance between AEU and AEA, we must turn our attention back to March 5, when the founders of AEU decided to build up their own independent mass organization at the school sites. From day one, their project, centered around the site liaison network, was far more organizationally ambitious than the grassroots groupings in West Virginia and Oklahoma. Though AEU leaders were not thinking in these terms at the time, they were in fact building something more like a proto-union than a rank-and-file caucus.

AEU's independent approach did not emerge from anti-union sentiment. To the contrary, almost all of the core nine were union members, and three (Harris, Wegela, and Fisher) were in fact elected AEA leaders at various levels. This organic connection to the union was a major differentiating factor from dynamics in Oklahoma. Fisher argues that "had there not been this membership kinship, there may have been more of a struggle with moving forward together because it could have been perceived as two competing organizations."

At the same time, AEU's core was well aware that only 25 percent of Arizona educators were union members. Wegela explains: "We all thought it was important to coordinate with the union, especially after first month. But we didn't go *through* the union, because it wouldn't have worked that way: AEA just didn't have the structure or the trust of our membership."

As Karvelis notes, Red for Ed's founders envisioned something bigger and politically broader: "One of the biggest reasons we established AEU was that it was clear to us that this all began on a grassroots level and was spreading on a grassroots level. So the thought of funneling people into the union didn't even cross our minds. Keep in mind that there's strong anti-union sentiment in Arizona. Before this movement, our coworkers generally said things like, 'AEA hasn't done anything, where has it been?' Others said that AEA was too political, too partisan. So it was really important for AEU not to have any partisan affiliation. We found a way to bring everyone on board the movement in a way the union couldn't."

Just as OEA leadership had done in Oklahoma, Arizona's top union leaders quickly took the initiative to reach out to rank-and-file organizers. Their first joint discussion took place on the evening of March 7, right after the massively successful Red for Ed day of action called by AEU. As was the case in the Sooner State, a tactical-political clash had led to considerable apprehension early on from both sides.

The main source of tension was AEA's announcement, during the Red for Ed mobilization earlier that day, of its endorsement of David Garcia, a Democratic candidate for governor. The *Arizona Republic* reported on the unexpected nature of the union's press conference: "In the middle of arguably the largest teacher demonstration in recent Arizona history Wednesday, the state's teachers' union essentially called a TV time out—to endorse a political candidate. And it didn't go over well for some."[9]

Wegela was one of these early critics. "I didn't trust the union leadership at first, especially because it endorsed David Garcia during our event," he notes. "It seemed like they were trying to steal our thunder, and it made it seem like Red for Ed had been established solely for the purpose of electing Garcia. The media really came after us—and the union—for that."

Things easily could have blown up on March 7. Indeed, the right wing's apparatus immediately sought to sow as much division as possible. Matthew Benson, a Republican political consultant, declared to the press that Garcia and AEA "effectively co-opted the (#RedForEd) movement today by choosing this day to announce their endorsement of Garcia for governor."[10]

It would have been simple for AEU leaders to have broken with the union at this moment. But instead, they responded to the Garcia incident by issuing a press release affirming that

9   Ricardo Cano, "Arizona Teacher Union's Governor Endorsement in Midst of Protest Criticized," *Arizona Republic*, March 9, 2018, azcentral.com.
10   Cited in Ibid.

Arizona Educators United was a nonpartisan organization that did not endorse any political candidate.

From March 7 onward, AEU and AEA leaders communicated through a joint Facebook chat and frequent conference calls. As the movement progressed, these relationships deepened, and most of the subsequent buildup actions and activities were jointly organized. Many local AEU organizers were simultaneously members of AEA—and sometimes even low-ranking officials of the latter.

AEU was strong in "people power" but low in resources. Fortunately, the union provided its office infrastructure, institutional legitimacy, research team, financial help (to print signs, rent speaker systems, etc.), and tactical advice without attempting to usurp the movement's leadership. "Teachers are the drivers of this bus; we're steering the struggle," noted Garelli when I first met her in April. "But the union is our parallel, and it has really supported us."

The US labor movement would be in a much better place if union leaders across the country adopted a similar stance. AEA President Joe Thomas, Vice President Marisol Garcia, and staff organizer Doug Kilgore deserve a lot of personal credit for solidifying a working alliance with Arizona's grassroots teacher leaders. Yet it would be a mistake to ignore the particular relationship of forces that made possible such a novel alliance. Put simply, the union leadership's consistent collaboration with its organized rank and file arose in response to AEU's exceptional strength and legitimacy. Unlike the teachers' unions in Oklahoma and West Virginia, AEA couldn't plausibly "go it alone" in the face of such an organizationally strong counterpart. Had a similarly influential grassroots structure existed in these other states, union officials there would likely have responded in the same way. As Karvelis explains, "AEA leaders saw the energy, they saw what we had created on the ground, and they said: 'You've done something that we haven't been able to do in twenty or thirty years.' And they saw that if they were to try to take the wheel, it would squash the movement."

Although AEA officials did not try to "take the wheel," they *did* use their considerable influence to encourage the movement to drive in a less risky direction. Indeed, much of the behind-the-scenes story of Red for Ed revolves around a long fight by AEU leaders—Dylan Wegela in particular—to overcome the union's hesitancy to support a work stoppage. Joe Thomas, in a poststrike panel for Los Angeles teacher unionists, was candid about the dynamic: "Unions—we're cautious because we have to be here on the next day . . . But [Arizona Educators United] wouldn't let us be cautious, which was good."

In contrast with Oklahoma, Arizona's call for a strike vote—let alone a strike—didn't come until very late in the game, mid April to be exact. Part of the reason for this, as we have seen, was that AEU militants like Garelli understood that it takes time to methodically build up to a work stoppage. "Maricopa was ready to go from day one," she recalls. "But this had to be a statewide shutdown."

This question of strike timing, however, was intertwined with an ongoing conflict over whether or not a strike was even feasible in Arizona. During the first six weeks of the movement, there were basically only two poles in this internal debate: Wegela and the AEA leadership. "From our first joint meeting on March 7 onwards," notes Wegela, "I was the only one bringing up the need for a strike—and I kept on getting shot down." His orientation on this question stemmed from his political conviction about the power of mass strikes: "I thought that a strike was the only way forward, because nothing else had worked. Electing Democrats didn't work—all across the country they've also cut school funds. But *strikes* work. My argument was basically: 'We can win. We're the gears of the machine, if we stop showing up, everything shuts down.' And even if we didn't end up winning everything, people needed to know they could do this, they needed to feel powerful. I wanted my coworkers and me to know what it felt like to say 'Hey boss, I'm not coming back until you fix this.'"

Apart from Wegela, most AEU leaders were initially skeptical about the prospects for a work stoppage in conservative Arizona, and/or hesitant to reject the tactical advice from their AEA allies. Garelli and Fisher told Wegela in private discussions that they agreed with his case for a strike. "We knew he had a real pulse on the feelings of our members, and we pushed for him to stand his ground," says Fisher. But when it came to speaking up at joint meetings with the union, they remained silent on this question.

AEU's hesitancy was buoyed by steady pressure from union leaders. In meeting after meeting, AEA officials argued against orienting to a strike. They raised three main objections. First, educators and community members in Arizona weren't yet ready for that type of action. Though this was often positively framed as an argument for more buildup activities, AEA's thrust was distinct from Garelli's specific concerns about timing. "We all definitely got the impression that the union, at least at first, was afraid of a walkout," notes Wegela. "They didn't seem to think people in Arizona would ever get on board. I'd ask them in meetings, 'How many liaisons do you think we need before we can go on strike?' Then we'd eventually hit that number and they still didn't want to do it."

Second, according to AEA leaders, educators wouldn't be able to get much out of the Republican-dominated legislature. It would be very dangerous to stage a walkout without a plan for "what would bring teachers back in" when they didn't win their demands. Wegela recalls that union leaders "kept saying that they had no faith that the Republicans would budge. My stance was that we had to force them to budge by shutting down the schools and staying out."

Finally, and relatedly, an unsuccessful walkout would jeopardize pro-education efforts in the upcoming November elections. In addition to their campaign to elect Garcia, AEA, in conjunction with some community allies, responded to the eruption of Red for Ed with the decision to put an initiative on the November ballot to fund education by raising income taxes for the rich.

At an April 19 press conference, union president Joe Thomas put forward an admirably sharp case for fixing public education by making the rich pay:

Here's the game that's played every year. Tax cut, tax cut, tax cut—and then a year later, there's no money for schools. We're tired of that game. Legislators need to reinvest dollars, the billion dollars that they stole from our students and schools over the past ten years. Let's roll back those corporate tax cuts—the people who can afford to pay should pay.

Without doubt, the "Invest in Ed" ballot campaign—officially announced to the public midway through the late-April walkout—was a major advance from the labor movement's traditional hesitancy to fight openly for progressive taxation. Yet the initiative's looming presence simultaneously served as one of AEA's main arguments against moving toward a potentially risky strike.

For all these reasons, Arizona's top union officials, despite their progressive political leanings, were on the whole *less* open to a walkout than those in Oklahoma. It's worth recalling that the Oklahoma Education Association had begun moving in the direction of a work stoppage even before West Virginia's strike began or Oklahoma's Facebook groups formed. In Arizona, it took a month and a half of pressure and sharp internal discussions to get union leaders on board.

An important turning point in the debate came when Wegela, Garelli, Arredondo-Aguirre, and Karbginsky attended the 2018 Labor Notes Conference, from April 6 to 8 in Chicago. Until this time, no one aside from Wegela had pushed for AEU and AEA to set a strike into motion. The conference, however, had a powerful impact upon AEU's participants. As Arredondo-Aguirre recalls: "For me, being completely new to this type of thing, it was hard to take sides in the debates about whether or not to strike. But Labor Notes really opened up my eyes because we all had a chance to talk to strike leaders from other states like West Virginia and Kentucky. They all kept telling us how impressed they were: 'You're way more organized than we ever were. If we could do a strike, you definitely can too.'"

Encouraged by these discussions, AEU's four participants in Chicago called the rest of the leadership team, hoping to get them on board with setting a date for a walkout. The majority of AEU leaders agreed with the plan—until a conference call with the union later that day. Garelli explains: "Basically, AEA leaders tried to squash the idea. They made it seem like we were only saying all this because we were being influenced by Labor Notes people. It was pretty condescending, and I told them so on that call. I said: 'I'm the only one here who has actual experience striking—I was in Chicago.'" But, to Wegela's chagrin, other AEU leaders eventually backed down in the face of the union's arguments.

Upon their return to Arizona, pressure from the ranks mounted, and internal debates continued to grow. Time was running out, since the legislative session was set to finish within a few weeks. Seeing the mounting anger and frustration from below, Wegela became increasingly worried that Red for Ed would fail to take action in time. "Dylan really had his finger on the pulse of things," notes Garelli. "He was site liaison coordinator, and he understood before the others that teachers weren't going to settle for less than a walkout."

Karvelis recalls that "the union brought in staff from [the National Education Association] to join us. Dylan was insistent: 'Our members want to walk—we have to honor what they want.' The NEA folks were trying to talk him back, to walk him back away from the cliff. But he was nailing it, sticking up for what he believed in, and he was beginning to turn the tide." Still, Wegela's efforts and the mounting rank-and-file calls for action were insufficient to swing the joint AEU-AEA calls.

The final breaking point in the debate came after 110,000 Arizonans participated in walk-ins on April 11. "We met as AEU right after that," recalls Wegela. "I argued *hard*. My main point was: 'What now? We need to escalate, and we can't just keep walking in. The only thing we can do now is walk out, or we'll miss the moment.'" This time, the AEU leadership not only agreed to the proposal to set a date for a walkout but also unanimously presented its decision to its AEA allies.

At certain junctures, the actions of movement leaders can be decisive for the course of mass struggle. It's impossible to say whether there would have been a unified statewide walkout without Dylan Wegela's stubborn internal push in this direction. Multiple AEU leaders were convinced it wouldn't have happened without him. In Karvelis's words: "Dylan was essential—I've never seen anything quite like it."

Had Wegela not won over AEU's core to the call for a walkout, Arizona's movement very well could have imploded as a result of demoralizing internal recriminations, or uncoordinated local walkouts by frustrated teachers unwilling to wait any longer.[11] But instead of holding yet another discussion over the feasibility of a walkout, the first AEU-AEA meeting after the April 11 walk-ins focused on the actual mechanics of calling one. Again, Garelli's experience of Chicago militancy proved to be invaluable. She recalls: "[President Joe Thomas]'s response to the walkout was now, 'Okay, but I can't do this kind of action without first asking my members.' So I proposed a strike authorization vote and I said: 'This is how we did it in Chicago.' When the union asked what this would actually look like, I explained to them that it was all laid out on Page 127 of the Labor Notes book *How to Jump-Start Your Union."*

On April 15, AEU leaders issued a call for a statewide strike vote. After multiple days of voting through secret paper ballots at each school site, AEU and union leaders made the results public at a joint press conference: of the more than 57,000 teachers and school staff who participated in the vote, 78 percent supported a work stoppage. On the basis of this bottom-up process of workplace democracy, and armed with a clear mandate for action, Red for Ed leaders announced that the walkout would begin on Thursday, April 26, and Friday, April 27.

---

11   Kentucky's inability to transition to an indefinite work stoppage at this very moment in April demonstrates the dangers of failing to strike when the iron is hot. Some of the reasons for the surprising absence of an extended work stoppage in Kentucky are touched on in Pranav Jani, "Where Will the Struggle Lead Kentucky Teachers?" *Socialist Worker,* April 13, 2018, social-istworker.org.

The Strike

As the strike day approached, Arizona's establishment ratcheted up its attacks on Red for Ed. In addition to intense redbaiting, numerous superintendents pressured their school employees to forgo participation in the strike.

In the days leading up to the strike, statewide superintendent Diane Douglas hit the media trail to threaten educators with the loss of their teaching certificates if they walked out: "A walkout is a nice term for it. It is a strike, plain and simple. And in Arizona, it is not legal for teachers to strike." She also denounced those school districts that were supporting Red for Ed, questioning "how a governing board can support an unlawful action legitimately."[12]

Another important expression of the Arizona political establishment's particular intransigence was that, unlike in both West Virginia and Oklahoma, it had still refused to pass a single legislative concession to avoid a strike. Indeed, had Arizona's educators not walked out in late April, it's possible that they would have won nothing.

On April 12, in response to the 110,000-strong walk-ins and AEU's announcement of an impending walkout, Ducey announced that he was increasing his proposal for a 1 percent teacher raise to 20 percent. There were numerous problems with this plan, including that it ignored support staff, would result in cuts to essential social services, and provided no

---

12   Joseph Flaherty, "Arizona Schools Chief Diane Douglas Threatens Teachers Over Strike, Says It's 'Not Legal,' " *Phoenix News Times,* April 24, 2018.

additional school funding. But, for all the flaws in Ducey's proposal, Republican lawmakers looked at a 20 percent pay raise as an exorbitant expense—and an unnecessary concession to rabble-rousers. On this basis, Republican lawmakers would continue to refuse to support the pay raise until midway through the strike.

The chronology of conservative politicians' public positions on the raise warrants careful attention, because after the walkout Governor Ducey and other Republicans attempted to paint themselves as friends of education who had granted the pay increase out of the goodness of their hearts. Indeed, AEU organizers foresaw that without a strong walkout, it was likely the Republican legislature would ultimately reject, or significantly reduce, Ducey's pay proposal—thereby allowing the governor to save face for his upcoming November reelection campaign, while simultaneously defeating and demoralizing the teachers.

It was in this context that a new debate emerged among AEU-AEA leaders. Once again a minority of one, Wegela argued hard for an indefinite strike aimed at winning both the pay *and* funding demands of AEU: "I felt we had the power and momentum to do a real strike like West Virginia, where they said: 'These are our demands, we're not going back to work until you meet them.' It would have been hard, definitely. But schools couldn't stay closed forever, so parents would have at some point turned on us, or on the politicians. And my sense was that folks would have turned on the politicians."

Most other AEU and AEA leaders felt that launching an indefinite strike was not worth the risk. Instead, they viewed the impending walkout primarily as a means to make sure Ducey's raise went through, ideally without the cuts to social services. Rather than attempt to stay out until all their main demands were met, it would make more sense to take a win and use the momentum to pivot to winning school funding through the Invest in Ed progressive taxation ballot initiative.

But whereas union leaders had floated the idea of a one-day walkout and were insistent about the dangers of an extended work stoppage, AEU's core envisioned staying out until a bill was signed. To quote Arredondo-Aguirre, "My view of the walkout was that we needed to keep it going until something was signed. But I knew we weren't going to get everything we wanted, not at first." Karvelis had a similar conception: "I didn't think we'd get all our demands through the walkout. But I thought we had to make sure the bill got through, and got through clean—we had to make sure it didn't get swept through on the backs of cuts to Medicaid recipients and kids with disabilities." These discussions, however, remained internal. For better or worse, most educators entered into the strike with no clear sense of how long it could last or what the baseline might be for a return to work.

Despite ongoing superintendent threats and a witch hunt against AEU leaders, the work stoppage begun on Thursday, April 26, was larger than anybody had anticipated. School was shut for over 850,000 students across the state—an extraordinarily high number given that almost a fifth of Arizona pupils are in charter schools. In the ninety-degree heat, roughly 75,000 educators and allies marched through the streets of Phoenix. Without the union's significant logistical and financial resources, it's unlikely that an event of this scale—the largest protest in Arizona history—could have been pulled off so smoothly.

During that afternoon's mass rally, AEU leaders came out swinging. Impervious to the red-baiting offensive, Wegela concluded his opening speech by yelling, "This is an education revolution!"

Karvelis was in top form, bringing the house down with a rousing call for collective struggle: "If we don't stand up for our kids, who will? [Crowd: 'Nobody!'] If we don't bring a change to this state, who will? If we don't stand up and bring a change, the people sitting in those chairs right now [inside the State House] will not do it. We have to be the ones to stand up and fight back in this moment, we have the power . . . And this movement—with the power of each and every one of us working together—will be the movement that goes down in history as the thing that changed education and the state of Arizona forever."

That same day, House Majority Whip Kelly Townsend issued a public statement threatening a class action lawsuit against strikers. And on Friday morning, the arch-reactionary Goldwater Institute sent letters to every district superintendent, declaring that they would be subject to lawsuits unless they immediately opened their schools.

Pressure from Republicans—and from conservative community members—was intensifying. On Friday, April 27, one teacher posted the following: "A woman in the grocery store today told me to go back to work—the children are being traumatized. We're being called hateful names, demeaned, and bullied. We're standing strong together, though." Some superintendents began to buckle, but the intimidation offensive generally failed to scare educators back to work. Despite the growing number of right-wing threats, educator turnout at Friday's rally was huge, and spirits remained high.

In response to the strikers' unforeseen resilience, at six o'clock Friday evening Ducey issued a press release stating that he had reached a deal with Republican lawmakers. Although the governor tried, cynically, to frame this as a personal triumph, he was ultimately forced to publicly acknowledge that the real tipping point was the strike: "The folks coming down to the state Capitol, making their voices heard, it helped me with other people I needed to get a budget passed, and that's why we're going to be able to introduce it on Monday and pass it soon after."[13]

In another significant concession, the proposed bill did not include Ducey's original plan to fund the raise by cutting social services.

In internal discussions, some union representatives raised the idea of calling partial victory, pivoting to Invest in Ed, and returning to work. But the AEU leadership team instead decided to poll liaisons over the weekend. The overwhelming response was that they, and their coworkers, wanted to come back to the capitol on Monday.

---

13   "'It's Official: We Have A Deal!' Gov. Ducey Announces Deal For 20% Teacher Raise," azfamily.com, April 27, 2018.

The walkout continued. Overall, momentum remained strong on Monday, which witnessed a turnout of roughly 50,000 at the capitol. At the same time, many district leaders began pushing hard to end the work stoppage; the precedent of a strike vote, however, made this task more difficult than it had been in Oklahoma. As Joe Thomas later explained, in most districts "superintendents were calling our local presidents asking if school was going to be shut the next day."

Tuesday afternoon brought the next big development. To the surprise of educators and the press, a joint AEU-AEA press conference announced that strikers would return to work on Thursday if the legislature passed Ducey's bill. Wegela had sharply opposed this move, arguing that it was necessary to let educators vote on whether or not to return. After the fact, AEU representatives agreed that it had been a mistake not to put the question up for a vote.[14]

At the same time, it was understandable that AEU's leadership felt it made sense to take ownership of the partial victory and pivot to the Invest in Ed campaign. Garelli explained, "There's been lots of pressure to return to work. And Ducey has been blasting the press all week, saying that he gave us a 20 percent raise. Lots of parents may not have responded well if we continued the walkout after the governor signed what they're being told is a big win for teachers."

Karvelis elaborates on this: "We all knew they were going to leave town after they passed the budget. So we would have

14 Rebecca Garelli, Noah Karvelis, Dylan Wegela, "The Outcome in Arizona," *Jacobin*, May 3, 2018, jacobinmag.com.

been left yelling at an empty building, trying to force a special session—to call that, you need a two-thirds vote from the legislature or a decision from the governor himself . . . The reality was that we didn't think we could get anything more from these legislators. Our thought was that if they would have conceded more to us, it would have already happened by now. Though they haven't done everything they're able to do, they've done all they're willing to do. So we thought it was time for a shift in tactics."

Though a minority of teachers wanted to stay out until all their demands were met, educators, in person and over social media, generally agreed that it made sense to return to school if Ducey's bill was signed. Nevertheless, most of these individuals were vocally angry that they were not consulted by the AEU leadership team. AEU's Facebook pages were riven by confusion and sharp debate. Wegela notes that "a majority of teachers were upset that we didn't give them a choice. I felt horrible about it; the whole thing started giving me anxiety attacks."

Momentum began to decline rapidly. Briefly, it seemed as if Arizona's walkout denouement might end up looking more like the implosion in Oklahoma. Wegela, however, was not prepared to give up. At this critical juncture, it was once again his efforts that proved to be the crucial link in the chain that pulled AEU's leadership, and then the movement, in a different direction. Wegela recounts the inauspicious origins of Wednesday's roller coaster of events: "Tuesday evening, right after our press conference, I was really upset about what we had done. So I went out for drinks with a friend of mine to vent—and to brainstorm ideas for what we could do. Over beers that night at the bar, we came up with the proposal that eventually turned things around: instead of going out without a fight, we could extend the strike and fire people back up by pushing to make amendments to the budget bill."

Wegela set the plan into motion early Wednesday morning on an AEU conference call with union leaders and Democratic legislators. The Democrats had set up the call to ask Red for Ed representatives how they should vote on Ducey's bill. "It was on that call," notes Wegela, "that we told them they needed to propose pro-education amendments, that would be paid for by taxing the rich." Specifically, the four amendments would (1) broaden the bill's definition of "teacher" to include all certified professionals; (2) cap student to teacher ratios at twenty-five to one; (3) cap student to counselor ratios at fifty to one; and (4) give a 10 percent raise to all support staff.

The Democrats accepted this proposal—at least in part. Wegela notes that "those Democratic lawmakers said they agreed, but they ended up watering down our original proposal by completely cutting all talk about funding mechanisms—I guess they didn't want to talk about taxing the rich. But it worked out okay because folks still ended up being super excited about the amendments."

Morale at the capitol was low on the morning of Wednesday, May 2. But it quickly began to turn back around after Arredondo-Aguirre posted a Facebook Live video update of Wegela and Garelli explaining the urgency of mobilizing for the four amendments and staying out until the bill was signed—even if this meant canceling school on Thursday or beyond: "If you can get down to the capitol tonight, *get here* . . . People [need to] put some pressure on the legislators . . . We need everybody here at the capitol until the budget is passed."

Educators responded enthusiastically. By the thousands, they streamed to the capitol, setting into motion one of the most sublime actions of the entire strike wave.

Garelli recalls the impact of the all-night capitol encampment: "That fight for the amendments, camping out all night, staying out another day on strike—that's what revived the energy. Honestly, it's what saved us. Without our amendment fight, the final budget process would have been a noose around our necks. That Wednesday night everybody—not only the teachers inside the chambers, but the entire state of Arizona watching online or on TV—witnessed Republican lawmakers vote down important amendment after amendment to improve our schools. People are still talking about this today. People saw with their own eyes who was responsible for the education crisis."

Wegela likewise stresses the importance of that final evening: "It was something special—it made it clear to educators that it was *their* actions, *their* power, that made the whole thing possible. And, honestly, I don't even know if the legislators would have ended up passing the raise if we hadn't kept the strike going until the end."

Apart from boosting morale, the amendment campout and strike extension were also key factors in making possible two major additional legislative victories. Faced with unprecedented public scrutiny, on Thursday, May 3, Republican lawmakers scrapped their proposed tax cuts and tax credits and dropped their attempt to prevent a referendum on vouchers from getting on the November 2018 ballot. Arizona educators did not win all their funding demands, but they could hold their heads high. Despite the long-standing weakness of Arizona's labor movement, they had built up an impressive level of collective power and wrested significant victories from one of the most reactionary state governments in the country.

Though Arizona's top union leaders were more hesitant than their grassroots counterparts, AEA played a crucial role in providing resources and legitimacy to the struggle. Seeing the Arizona Education Association's considerable impact in major wins for educators, approximately 2,500 new members joined the union during spring 2018—a number higher than anywhere else in the red state revolt. At the same time, it's unquestionable that Arizona Educators United was the organization most responsible for making this historic strike possible. It was the tireless work of each liaison and every member of the AEU core that collectively drove the struggle forward. And at the center of this rank-and-file upsurge were Garelli, Karvelis, and Wegela.

None of these young teachers sought recognition for their contributions. But they deserve it. Karvelis was speaking of past social movements when he remarked that "radicals and anti-capitalists have a big role to play—if you look at history, you see that those folks are often at the forefront of labor struggles." Arizona showed that this insight remains no less true today than it was fifty or a hundred years ago.

Conclusion

Before they occur, successful strikes appear impossible to most people. Afterward, they seem almost inevitable. And underlying both of these mistaken assumptions is a failure to account for the agency of organizers.

Socialists, of course, didn't create the 2018 education movements single-handedly. Without the active support of the trade unions and the activation of tens of thousands of educators, none of these victories would have been possible. Nor were radicals responsible for the material grievances that propelled these struggles forward. Contrary to the ravings of Republican leaders, class struggle is not produced by "outside agitators"; instead, it's the result of an inherent structural antagonism between those who have to sell their labor to survive and the few who profit off this labor.

But as we have seen, the successes of the spring 2018 work stoppages often hinged on interventions by experienced workplace militants. Without accounting for their behind-the-scenes decisions and debates, it's impossible to make sense of the divergent outcomes in West Virginia and Arizona, on one hand, and Oklahoma, on the other. Though red state educators operated in conditions not of their own choosing, they really did make their own history.

Instead of treating the recent educators' strikes and the massive growth of the socialist movement since 2016 as two separate and distinct processes, this chapter has shown that labor militancy and political radicalism advanced hand in hand. Had it not been for the resurgence of socialist politics set into motion by Bernie Sanders's primary run, the course of struggle in these states would have looked very different.

And all signs point to the deepening of this symbiotic relationship in the coming years. To quote Oklahoma DSA activist Jorge Roman-Romero: "I may be very optimistic, but I think we've entered a new historic period after the Bernie Sanders campaign and now these strikes. There is a new working-class political pole—and people, even those who are not on the Left, are becoming very receptive to it. To improve people's living and working conditions urgently requires major challenges to the system. And that can't be brought by the mainstream. We have the momentum, it's just a matter of getting organized. Of course, effectively organizing isn't easy for a young group like us. But we can see the opportunities. Ordinary people aren't dumb; they just need to see an alternative."

To be sure, it is not inevitable that the growth of socialist organizations will result in the rebirth of a militant labor movement. Apart from the fact that most young activists today are still not convinced of the centrality of workplace organizing and labor unions, it's also the case that the presence of experienced radicals in an industry doesn't automatically enable collective militancy.

Conditions need to be ripe—mass strikes can't just be willed into being. Timing is key, as exemplified in the development of the spring 2018 upsurge: rank-and-file teachers in Oklahoma and Arizona were able to ride, and give expression to, the outpouring of excitement and enthusiasm generated by West Virginia's recent victory.

Different contexts also create distinct tactical obstacles and opportunities. The relationship of forces between the rank and file, union officials, and management varies greatly across industry and region in the United States. There were important contextual reasons why West Virginia and Arizona's radicals, despite their very small numbers, were able to play such an exceptionally outsized role at a moment of crisis and upsurge. In part because of the legal prohibition on public sector strikes and the absence of strong collective-bargaining mechanisms, there existed a leadership vacuum that a small militant minority was able to fill. At the same time, the fact that these red states' labor officialdoms were relatively weak, and that the Democrats were out of power, helps explain why radicals were effective at pressuring the unions into supporting illegal work stoppages.

By way of contrast, much larger groups of leftist educators in cities like Chicago or Los Angeles have had to spend years patiently working within their unions to develop strong caucuses capable of overcoming the entrenched officialdom. Only through such protracted efforts could they transform these organizations into democratic fighting bodies capable of building workers' power within the existing collective bargaining parameters. Effective struggle against the private sector's corporate giants will likely require even-deeper organizing and greater strategic clarity.

Though the West Virginia and Arizona strikes do not provide a timeless political model that is replicable for the entire country, one lesson is clear: if we want to win, leftists need to start organizing at our workplaces and in our unions, when we're lucky enough to have them. As the experience of the red state revolt illustrates, the revival of organized labor is inseparable from the project of rebuilding a militant minority.

No one has any illusions that it will be easy to reestablish an influential Left rooted in a fighting working class. This will require patient organizing over many years. Our enemies are powerful—and we'll certainly experience many defeats along the way. But never underestimate the ability of working people to turn the world upside down.

EPILOGUE: LOOKING AHEAD

It remains to be seen whether educators in West Virginia, Arizona, Oklahoma and beyond can channel the energy of the 2018 strikes into sustained organizational and political power over the coming years.

But there are good reasons to be optimistic about the prospects for continued education militancy and labor revitalization in the United States. Just as defeats in struggle lead to demoralization and resignation, victories tend to beget more victories. The spring 2018 movements radically shifted the national narrative about who is responsible for the education crisis. A sustained surge of successful school strikes in the coming period could turn back the neoliberal tide in public education, boost the trade union movement, and potentially spark workers' militancy across the public and private sectors. The powers that be understand this—which is why they are likely to do everything possible to prevent such a possibility from becoming a reality.

Across the country, co-optation and repression should be expected on scales as yet unseen. Within West Virginia,

Oklahoma, and Arizona, the forces of reaction have already clearly demonstrated their increased political resolve. Dead set on defending their wealth and demoralizing working people, they're fighting harder than ever to defeat educator battles around the strikes' outstanding demands. The corporate-bought removal of the Invest in Ed initiative from the ballot by the Arizona Supreme Court in August 2018 was only one—egregiously anti-democratic—expression of this well-financed commitment to win "round two."

Given the power of the ruling rich and the contingencies of mass struggle, trying to guess if and where strikes will continue to spread is no simple task. And in crucial ways, to do so would misidentify the strategic question at stake. The basic problem with such predictions is that what happens in the coming period depends in large part upon what we choose to do. In a post-Oklahoma discussion about the prospects for the strike wave's continuation, Jane McAlevey made an important point:

> I don't like the term "wave." Everybody uses it, but to me as an organizer I see that workers build worker agency through struggle. A wave sounds like a mysterious phenomenon that we don't have any control over. It implies that the wave can suddenly go back out to sea, regardless of what we do. I don't believe that. I believe that it's up to us to figure out how to continue building powerful movements right now.[1]

---

1   Jane McAlevey and Eric Blanc, "A Strategy to Win," *Jacobin*, April 18, 2018, jacobinmag.com.

That's why learning about the 2018 red state rebellions is so politically important: to fight effectively for a better future requires an accurate understanding of the past. Illegal mass strikes did more to revive the trade union movement, and to force concessions from employers, than decades of electing and lobbying liberal Democrats. Though these politicians and their allied labor leaders may tack to the left under pressure from below, neither are interested in articulating—or consistently implementing—the main strategic lessons of the recent upsurge.

Fortunately, many strike participants have drawn their own conclusions. West Virginia teacher Carrena Rouse put it well: "I'd like to give God credit for moving the politicians' hearts, but unless they raise the tax on natural gas to fix PEIA, I think we might have to go back on strike."

The red state revolt was a historic step forward for working people. But ultimately it was just one early battle in what will certainly be a much-longer war to save our schools and transform the United States into a country where government policy is determined by human needs, not corporate profits.

It's impossible to know how this conflict will play out. Influential business interests and their political proxies remain committed to dismantling our unions and privatizing public services. As the social safety net and living standards decline, Trumpism and racist scapegoating can appear to many as the only alternative to the status quo.

But if working people cohere themselves politically and reverse this reactionary drive, there's little reason to assume that they'll stop there. Depending on the course of struggle in the coming years, all sorts of transformative demands and projects that today seem far-fetched could become realizable.

Successful strikes have an extraordinary power to raise working-class expectations. From winning comprehensive labor law reform, to building an independent workers' party, to decommodifying health care, transportation, and energy production—nothing is off the table. The Koch brothers are right to be worried.

ACKNOWLEDGEMENTS

This book would not have been possible without the political wisdom, hospitality, and support of teachers and comrades from across the country. I'd like to thank, first and foremost, all educators who went on strike in 2018 and especially the dozens who welcomed me into their schools, meetings, and homes, and who agreed to be interviewed for this book.

A very special thanks goes out to my family, Emily Comer, Jay O'Neal, Nicole and Matt McCormick, Cathy Kunkel, Ted Boettner, Stephen Noble Smith, Dan Taylor, Olivia Morris, Stephanie Price, Royce Sharp, Xavier Doolittle, Dylan Wegela, Rebecca Garelli, Noah Karvelis, Robert Kirsch, Jane McAlevey, Ellen David Friedman, Charlie Post, Dan DiMaggio, Rebecca Tarlau, Lois Weiner, Joe Burns, Jeff Goodwin, Vivek Chibber, Bhaskar Sunkara, Micah Uetricht, Shawn Gude, and all the *Jacobin* comrades, Ryan Bruckenthal, Patrick Dedauw, Yael Bridge, Yoni Golijov, Sarah H., Jason Farbman, Dana Blanchard, Ashley Smith, Jessie Muldoon, Marsha Niemeijer, and Ben Mabie and the whole Verso team.